F

Why We Watch

Killing the Gilligan Within

Dr. Will Miller
Nick at Nite's Teletherapist

A FIRESIDE BOOK
Published by Simon & Schuster

FIRESIDE
Rockefeller Center
1230 Avenue of the Americas
New York, NY 10020

Designed by Bonni Leon-Berman

Manufactured in the United States of America

10   9   8   7   6   5   4   3   2   1

Library of Congress Cataloging-in-Publication Data

Miller, Will, Dr.
    Why we watch : killing the Gilligan within / Dr. Will Miller.
    p.   cm.
    "A Fireside book."
    1. Television programs—Humor.   I. Title.
PN6162.M495   1996
791.45'75'0207—dc20   96-42045
                                                          CIP

ISBN 0-684-83106-6

The views expressed in this book are those of the author
and not Nick at Night.

For Sally. Even in the noisiest comedy clubs,
I could always hear her laughter.

CONTENTS

Part II

Teletherapy's Profiles of the 30 Most Psychologically Misunderstood Television Programs in History

We Are All Three Stooges   113

ACKNOWLEDGMENTS

As with every book, there are many people responsible for its appearance. In this case they include:

First of all, my wife Sally, our kids, and our family, for their love. These are the people who have believed in me without ceasing and have patiently endured my seventeen years in show business;

Jeff Schwartz, manager extraordinaire, who has given expert vision for my career, as well as loyal friendship. He and Ian Heller continue to keep me on track, encouraged, and solvent. I simply could not have done this without them;

My collaborators at Nick at Nite, who have also become my good friends, especially the brilliant Tom Hill. I am so grateful to Paul Ward, Larry Jones, Rich Cronin, and the most creative group of professionals I have ever known;

Trish Todd, my editor at Simon & Schuster and new friend, who along with Aviva Goode made the entire process a delight;

My parents, brothers, and sisters, who laughed out loud, especially Stephen who talked me into starting my comedy career;

My comedy colleague Grover Silcox, who helped me start the "Dr. Will" ball rolling;

William Morris super agents Dan Strone and, especially, my friend Henry Reisch, whom I trust;

My analyst Dr. Janet Bachant, who gave me my useable, adult personality;

And to Abe Vigoda and his brilliant work on the television classic, *Fish,* which triggered my discovery of Teletherapy.

FOREWORD

I believe that television, when used in the right way, can be a tool for personal well-being and psychological health. As I noted in a recent address to the International Symposium on Classic TV in Geneva, Wyoming, "I believe the American television rerun is a pathway to personal peace." While this might appear to be a hopelessly bold assertion, this book will prove it is true! Television has often been scrutinized using the lens of psychoanalytic theory. Even Freud was said to have been fascinated by the concept of television media, often caught staring blankly at a small hollow box behind his desk.

Television is simultaneously a mirror of our society and a powerful force that shapes culture. By looking at our television heritage we retrieve rich insight into our collective identity. In essence, television reruns provide a window into the American psyche, and as such, can be used as a therapeutic tool.

What is not often discussed are the repercussions of television programs that are not deemed controversial. What about the seemingly innocuous fare that many of us grew up watching? Is there any negative impact from long-term exposure to *Mister Ed?* What does a steady diet of *The Brady Bunch* do to a human psyche? Are we hurt by watching *Scoobie Doo* for ten years? What occurs within someone's personality as a result of seeing *Shindig?* You are about to find out. For you are about to enter into the exciting new world of Teletherapy, a new healing technique I have developed for Nick at Nite to serve you, the neurotic viewer.

By reading this book and following the program outlined within, many of your personal problems will simply melt away. This book will assist you in untangling the complex web of television influences that helped shape your evolving personality. It is a self-help resource showing you a new way to use television to better your life. By using the award-winning techniques of Teletherapy, you can watch your way to wellness. I promise you, you will learn a great deal more than you anticipated, perhaps more than you wanted. Forge ahead. You can be healed through television.

So there you have it. Good luck and God speed.

Your pal,

Dr. Will Miller

PART I

The Miracle of Teletherapy

CHAPTER 1

The Miracle of Teletherapy

Do You Need Teletherapy?

Are you in doubt that our society, and every individual in it, is in dire need of inner healing? Do you question the notion that stress is eroding the shoreline between civilization and the ocean of madness? Can you deny that you, your family, and the entire community we call America are both personally and collectively dysfunctional? Will you look yourself in the eye and contend that your inner child is in no need of nurturing and most of your key dreams have not been shattered?

Take This Quiz

1. Have you ever fantasized that you were a character on a television show?
2. When in a life-threatening situation, have you ever wondered what MacGyver would do?
3. Have you ever publicly denied watching Sally Jessy Raphael or Jenny Jones?
4. If held at gunpoint, could you name at least two members of the Jetson family?
5. Could you enjoy *Baywatch* even if the sound on your television was broken?

If you answered any of these questions yes, even if you subtly leaned toward a positive response, it is obvious that you have been deeply affected, and probably wounded, by the television you watched. As such, I can state unequivocally that you are in need of *Teletherapy!* To reject this means that you are in the iron grip of denial. You are shut off from reality if you are not in total agreement with this undeniable premise. It is possible that you are psychotic.

Did you grow up watching a lot of television? Do you currently find any enjoy-

Seen through the eyes of television, these photos represent American culture 1956 and 1996. Look closely at them. Can there be any doubt that we need to study these symbols? Only Teletherapy can fairly lead the discussion into the meaning of these pictures.

ment in watching television? If the answer is yes, then be of good cheer. You have come to the right place for help. This book will completely heal you. By reading this book and participating in the television-based activities it prescribes, you will smash through your denial and completely change your life. Further, I can personally guarantee that, if you will meticulously apply the principles of Teletherapy, you will become financially successful beyond your wildest dreams within thirty-six months!

If you brush these claims off as being exaggerated nonsense, you're right. Nothing in life is easy. Let me assure you that engaging in the Teletherapeutic process is indeed quite demanding. You will have to think deeper thoughts than you ever imagined. You will have to feel your emotions at full throttle. You will stretch; you will grow; you will perspire profusely. Along the way you will overcome habits and instincts that have been part of your identity since you were a small child. You will have to confront your assumptions about many things—in particular, your ideas and opinions about your most beloved television heroes. What I will propose to you in this book about the television shows and characters you have always loved will be emotionally wrenching. Be prepared! You will undoubtedly experience emotional pain, a sinking feeling of uncertainty, even chronic headaches. But it will all be worthwhile. Stick with it and you will not believe the results.

So what are you waiting for? Let's get busy! Let's get healed!

What Is Teletherapy?

Teletherapy is a new method of psychological healing based on the careful analysis of prescribed television viewing. It is a fusion of the words television and therapy, and so exactly describes what it does. The name television comes from the Greek *tele,* which means distant or far off, and the Latin word *visio,* meaning to see. Television means seeing something from a far distance. Thus the term "Teletherapy" means to be healed from far away. Note that since "Teletherapy" is a combination of Latin and Greek, it is a metaphor for itself! Just as the word fuses the Roman with the Greek, the classic culture with the contaminated culture, so too Teletherapy merges the high art of psychoanalytic psychotherapy with the murky bottom of America's popular trash culture.

So even though I am physically in my office at the Nick at Nite Think Tank and Research Laboratories in Lafayette, Indiana, I am actually in the process of healing you from far away through the indirect medium of television. Is it any wonder that I often refer to this process as the "miracle of Teletherapy?" This, my friends, is exactly what it is—a miracle!

Five Common Signs Indicating a Need for Teletherapy Treatment

1. In normal conversations, you speak as if from a script, always feeling that you are awaiting your turn to deliver a line. In severe cases, this might also include spending time preparing your verbal input for a routine social interaction.
2. During sitcoms, a variety of physical symptoms emerge including unexpected swooning, persistent ringing sounds in the ears, involuntary tics such as lip twitching and hand-washing motions, and a fear of phantom limb pain.
3. In social situations, initiating inappropriate and emotionally charged conversations about television characters. For instance, you begin openly weeping while describing the suffering of fugitive Dr. Richard Kimble.
4. Agitation while watching public broadcasting.
5. Making more than three calls within six months to *America's Most Wanted* to offer information.

The Power of Television

Far from being a waste of time, television is a powerful tool—if used in the right way. In essence, you can literally "watch your way to wellness."[1] Teletherapy flatly rejects every and all previous theories and assumptions that television is bad for you. Nonsense! Is a scalpel bad? Only if used for the wrong purpose. If used as intended, the scalpel cuts and slices for healing. If it is used for dicing, it is in the hands of an amateur. I think you get the point.

[1] Senior Teletherapist Ronald Gill, speech to Classic TV Symposium, Buenos Aires, Argentina, July 1994.

Don't be fooled by the superficial criticism of television. There are many misinformed pundits who see in television an easy scapegoat for all social ills. This is invalid. The proponents of such theories are either poorly educated in the metaphysical sciences, unschooled in the rudiments of Teletherapy, or even suffer from a serious adjustment disorder. In a highly under-reported research project at a major junior college, an analysis of television criticism concluded that over 48 percent of those who wrote more than one article blaming television for social problems showed almost all of the symptoms associated with alien abduction and surgery.[2] Enough said.

If you watch television with the assistance of Teletherapy, everything about your personality will change forever. In fact, I can personally guarantee that your psychological problems will simply melt away. We see television as a cornucopia spilling over with profound lessons for life, and Teletherapy is a treatment that has been called a "balm to the soul."[3] The messages every show contains are powerful reflections of human social and cultural reality. You can learn just about anything you want. You can gain insight into every imaginable topic. You can overcome any problem you have with the proper use of television. If only you will try. Shed your inhibitions. Be the person you are intended to become! Chin up! Remember, today is the first day of the rest of your life! So turn on the television set!

My Promise and Your Pledge

This book is divided into several chapters each dealing with a major dimension of mental health and Teletherapy's response to it. As you progress on your healing path you will address such diverse and vital issues as self-esteem, anger, fear, sexuality, love, even the paranormal. I will also describe how you can use the principles of Teletherapy to become rich. Imagine cruising across your town's lake aboard your yacht. Your neighbors are green with envy! All this because you learned how to use television properly. By the end of this book, your life will be changed forever.

[2] "An Analysis of TV Criticism & Alien Abductions" (publication pending), Addams J.C., N. Berlin, Germany, H. Dukes, Ed., January 1995.

[3] Dennis Rodman, discarded note recovered by Cheryl Nifoussi, Olive Garden waitress, San Antonio, Texas, July 11, 1994.

Teletherapy Breathing Exercise

Before engaging in any of the exercises suggested in this book, it is recommended that you begin with the following breathing exercise. This technique is taken from my book *Tele-Zen: Watching TV from the East Side of the Den.* (CAUTION: Do not attempt this exercise if you have a history of bronchial or inner ear weakness. It is not recommended for children. If you feel the beginnings of a fever, stop immediately. Consult your physician if you are unsure.)

1. Take off your shoes and jewelry. Stand with your hands behind your head, fingers interlocking. Expel all the air from your lungs and hold this position for as long as possible. Repeat this until you feel unsteady.
2. Hold a cold compress on your forehead for a full minute.
3. Beginning with the top of your head, eliminate all tension in each part of your body as you listen to Yanni or Enya music.
4. Bathe or shower vigorously. If facilities are unavailable, aggressively sponge bathe.
5. Towel dry and resume the recommended activity.

And with this, I would like to share with you my Four Promises of Teletherapy, as well as the Teletherapy Honor Pledge. The Four Promises I make to you are:

1. I promise that television can cure at least 40 percent of your core psychological illnesses;
2. I promise that you will firmly grasp your personal identity in terms of a television character (you will be able to say, for example, "I am a Shemp with a Gilligan rising," or "I have a repressed Emily Hartley cowered by a flamboyant, over-arching Sue Ann Niven");
3. I promise that you will either surpass your personal goals for career and romance, or you will change these goals as a result of Teletherapy;
4. I promise that you will become rich through the use of Teletherapy within three years!

And now the pledge. Stand up. With your remote control in one hand and a copy of *TV Guide* in the other, state the following out loud in front of a witness:

> I, (*state your name*), pledge to adhere to the principles of Teletherapy as closely as humanly possible. I will use them to grow, become psychologically healthy, and, where possible, to better my lot in society. Furthermore, I vow to never misuse these techniques to the harm of myself or another person. And I pledge to always use these strategies to help rebuild the psychological fabric of America, even if it means turning in loved ones to the proper authorities. So help me (*state your higher power*). Amen, Amen.

Clearly you are now ready for the curative possibilities of this miraculous new technique. Good luck and God speed. Be sure to write to me at Nick at Nite to share your Teletherapeutic experiences. (I will expect the letter to be sent from your yacht!)

CHAPTER 2

Teletherapy: Basic Concepts

What You Need to Know

We must first determine your beginning level of knowledge of Teletherapy. (If you are a certified Teletherapist, have attended a Teletherapy course within the last six months, or have watched at least two-thirds of the Teletherapy infomercial you can skip this section.) What is your knowledge of fundamental therapeutic terms and concepts? Take this brief pre-test to certify your starting point.

1. You're a passenger in a car traveling a high rate of speed. Murray Slaughter and Gomez Addams are with you. Would you feel safer if the driver is Murray or Gomez?
2. Would Mr. Peabody have more of a personality clash with Rocky or Bullwinkle?
3. Joe Friday or Steve McGarrett: Which one is more likely to snap and why?

1. Murray and Gomez: Who Is Sicker and Why?

As you hurtle down the highway at over ninety miles per hour, you are naturally fearing for your life. You are completely dependent on the ability and the sanity of the driver. If you said you would feel better with Murray Slaughter driving the car, YOUR LIFE IS IN DANGER! It is apparent you do not realize that Murray is a depressed man. His sense of self-worth is quite low. In other words, his will to live is far weaker than you might think. Thus he is less fearful about the thought of his own death. All this is unconscious, of course. He has no conscious awareness that he has active fantasies about "shuffling off this mortal coil." [1]

---

[1] Charles Winchester to Major Margaret Hoolihan as quoted from a play by William Shakespeare.

This is why it should be a comfort to see Gomez Addams at the wheel. Gomez, despite his eccentricities and bizarre notions, is nonetheless a man full of the joy of life. He remains deeply infatuated with his wife, the lush Morticia, and devoted to his two peculiar children. His investment career moves along swimmingly, and he has a robust sense of his own expansive destiny. No, Gomez shows no signs of depression and appears to be the last person to put himself at risk in a suicidal car ride. Don't be taken in by outward appearances. Teletherapy would

suggest that you are better off depending on the off-center Gomez Addams than the more subtly unbalanced Murray Slaughter.

What about you? Do you drive fast and dangerously? Are your loved ones fearful of how you drive? Perhaps you are taking inappropriate risks with your life. Your reckless driving could well be a sign of a faulty will to live. Change this today! How? Continue reading and incorporate the principles of Teletherapy's healing treatment techniques into your life.

So as you can see, you have only read a few pages and Teletherapy may have already saved the lives of you and your family!

2. Mr. Peabody Gets Irritated: The Shadow Knows

Have you ever noticed that certain people bother you more than others? Of course you have. For each of us, there are certain individuals whose very being is a source of deep stress and anxiety. Whenever they walk into the room, psychological bile rises in your psyche (if real bile rises in your throat, this could indicate an organic illness).

And what about the reverse situation? Have you yourself ever been a source of persistent irritation to another person? Certainly you have. If you cannot name one person who is repelled by your presence, ask family members and friends to help you identify those individuals who have spoken hatefully about you. Every person has experienced the difficulty of rubbing someone the wrong way or realizing that someone becomes agitated whenever you are around them.

Have you ever asked yourself what is at the root of these hostile feelings? Probably not. In psychology, the term coined by the great Carl Jung is the "shadow."[2] It refers to the phenomenon of seeing qualities in this irritating other

person that you yourself possess but try very hard to hide. For example, if you become very agitated around someone who is aggressive, it probably indicates that you repress your own strong hostility. Seeing their anger reminds us about our own rage, so we become uncomfortable. Very often the qualities we work so hard to project to the outside world are a reaction to some very strong impulses we actually have in the exact opposite direction! Isn't this fantastic to know? Take any quality you project, and you can surmise that deep inside you there are unconscious urges to do and be the reverse!

So taking this fascinating notion of the shadow, let's consider the question above. What qualities does Mr. Peabody have? What image does he project to the world? If you said intellectual, you are quite right. What is the opposite of intellectual? Stupid, dense, thick. And who does this best describe—Rocky or Bullwinkle? Yes, of course, the obtuse Moose! Thus Bullwinkle, with his open display of moronia, complete with the voice of an imbecile, would expose to Mr. Peabody the part of himself that is also a dull-witted ass. Bullwinkle is Mr. Peabody's shadow!

---

[2] The great Swiss psychoanalyst first used this term to his sister over a light lunch at a spa in Germany.

Who Is Your Shadow?

Discreetly videotape your most bitter enemy for at least two hours. Study the tape and make a list of at least three of their most significant qualities that you find most intolerable. Then use this list to search out these same qualities buried in your own unconscious. For example, here is a "Shadow List" that was developed by Ron Gogul, Teletherapy patient:

"Sandy's most horrendous personal qualities include:

1. sloppiness
2. poor breath
3. body odor

I find these characteristics to be unbearable!"[3]

This list told his Teletherapist that Ron himself had a deep, unconscious desire to allow his personal hygiene to deteriorate. The Teletherapist rightfully recommended viewing *The Odd Couple* for nine hours a week for three months. As a result the tension between the two completely dissipated, and they are now close personal friends. In fact, they started an *Odd Couple* Fan Club at work and have taken several junkets together.[4]

If you annoy someone and are their shadow, provide them with a videotape of yourself along with the instructions above.

3. Joe and Steve: Tightwires!

As viewers, we experience psychological relief by watching police action-dramas. The reason is that, in real life, we often feel powerless in the face of naked aggression by hoodlums who act out their antisocial impulses. In real life, for instance, if we happen upon some crime in progress, our good judgment about self-preservation makes it unlikely that we will actually intervene. We might have a fleeting fantasy about donning a costume and beating up the perpetrator, but this is usual-

---

[3] Sandy is Ron's supervisor at a small linoleum manufacturing plant in southern Vermont.
[4] Tragically, both Ron and Sandy were killed in a drill press incident at their plant.

ly an unrealistic aspiration.[5] Most of us experience the painful frustration of our impotence. We are enraged, but we can do nothing about it.

This rage echoes back to our earliest experiences as an infant when we might have become enraged that our basic needs were not being met, but were powerless to act on this rage. When we see lawbreakers, we transfer that infantile rage onto the perpetrator. It becomes deeply satisfying to us personally when we see them get their just due. Because this is such a deep-seated impulse, we take it personally when someone gets away with something. In this context, people like Joe Friday and Steve McGarrett become our hero-parent. Their relentless pursuit of justice and the personal outrage they display quells our own agitation. Police dramas serve a useful purpose in easing this percolating anxiety.

But what is the cost to Joe and Steve? What is it doing to their inner selves? Is the cost too high? Certainly the pressures of always assuming responsibility for overcoming evil are enormous. So let's look at these two men of distinguished valor. Of the two, which one seems to have a more active private life of recreation? If you said Joe Friday, you are completely wrong and you have just made an

impaired judgment. (If this is a consistent pattern in your life, it would be unwise for you to seek a career in law enforcement or the hazardous material–handling industry.)

If you said Steve McGarrett, you are quite observant. Steve often takes time to surf, date, and hang-glide. In contrast, Joe Friday lives a more sparse existence. He usually reports very little interest in outside activities. His formal dress and demeanor would make him stand out in a crowd and evoke more suspicion among strangers. He also has a penchant for engaging in police activity on his off-duty time. Can there be any doubt that, even on his off-duty time, if Joe saw a

---

[5] If you have actually tried this strategy, you might want to seek help for your impulse control difficulties.

person parking in a handicapped spot at the grocery store he would intervene and compel the offender to move or face arrest? Add to this the fact that his smoking would dissuade a significant number of friendships and suitors, and you are looking at a man who is more socially isolated than he ought to be.

The result of this difference is that Steve McGarrett has built into his life many more opportunities to seek relief from the stress of his work. He is far less likely to decompensate into derangement than Sgt. Joe. While there is always the hope that Joe will change his ways and find some healthy diversions, there is as yet no indication of his doing so. Based on his present patterns, he is far more likely to experience a psychological meltdown into madness. If you saw this, you are to be congratulated. You have demonstrated keen Teletherapeutic insight.

A Simple New Language!

Perhaps the greatest gift of Teletherapy is that it can give you a vivid, easily understood description of the human personality. Suddenly, you have a mental picture that does not require an expert's knowledge of psychology to comprehend. This is a crucial tool for the nonprofessional. For example, if I said that an individual had "an adjustment disorder complicated by a clear, but unspecified Axis II personality diagnosis, along with weight loss due to irritable bowel syndrome," you might be overwhelmed. But if I chose instead to say this person has "Barney Fife Syndrome," his condition becomes instantly clear to you.

Teletherapy makes complex psychological issues easily comprehensible to even the most intellectually limited individual—or better said—to even those suffering with "Goober Complex." See how clear it becomes? Let's use a practical example.

The Gumby Dynamic

How do you see Gumby? Is he taffy? Is he putty? Is he plastic? (If you thought metal or wood, you might want to consider being tested for perceptual difficulties.) Clearly Gumby is a boy whose unique shape and substance are central to his identity. He is quite flat in shape, suggesting a two-dimensionality. Lack of depth is one of his most significant features. Being a putty or taffylike substance, it means he is simultaneously pliable and, disturbingly, squashable. His makeup indicates a lack of inner substance. In essence, others can stretch and reshape

Gumby. He frequently relies on a farm animal, his horse Pokey, for wisdom and advice. He is thus not a well-educated or intellectually mature individual. But although he is something of a simpleton, he is nonetheless a kind, civil, and well-disciplined adolescent.

Now let's talk about you. Think about the description above. Do any of these characteristics describe you? Are you a two-dimensional dullard who can be shaped or crushed by outside forces, all the while feeling a childlike inability to defend yourself? If so, you have Gumby Syndrome. This is great news, because you have now defined your condition, which is the first step in changing your life. See how quickly Teletherapy begins the healing process?

Yes, Teletherapy confronts you with deep questions, which need deep answers. Are you deep enough? Probably not. No one is without many years of insight. Teletherapy takes years off the search. You will become deep more quickly than you ever imagined.

Television: Both Friend and Killer

Like any household equipment, television can be a valued convenience or an instrument of death. As Gunnar Ollsen has stated, "only the refrigerator has killed more people."[6] For most people, however, the television's role in their lives lies somewhere in between these extremes. As such, we must be on guard for the early signs of television-related problems. There are many emotional, social, and psychological illnesses that are unique to television viewers. For starters, here is a list of several maladies that are rooted in poor television viewing. It is appalling that these have never been defined or described in past self-help literature. Take note of these serious conditions to see if you or someone you know is a silent victim.[7]

Television Separation Stare When unable to be near a television, the victim is so anxious he becomes transfixed by any object whose shape resembles a television. In extreme cases, victims have been known to sit motionless in front of a microwave oven and even the dark opening of a dog house.

---

[6] Teletherapist and Senior Technical Engineer, Gunnar's Appliances, Framingham, Massachusetts.

[7] This is by no means an exhaustive list. At last count, Nick at Nite researchers have identified over 340 separate illnesses and syndromes associated with television and needing the specialized treatment of Teletherapy.

Cartoon Phonics Disorder Over-identification with animated characters with speech impediments creates chronic phonetic difficulty.

Ryan Screen Fungus[8] A rare condition whereby the victim watches TV immediately after invigorating physical activity and while still perspiring. Such prolonged viewing in damp clothing triggers a skin fungus.

TV Inhalant Disorder A severe condition characterized by an addiction to breathing dust particles visible in the light of the television screen.

Cable Wire Phobia A condition of extreme fear that the cable system will malfunction and cut the victim off from viewing. A related condition is known as SDAC ("Satellite Dish Aiming Compulsion"), which describes a compulsion to constantly realign a satellite dish for better reception. These conditions often require hospitalization during thunderstorms.

Simpsons Movement Disorder Bonding with the characters on *The Simpsons* becomes so undivided the victim begins walking in the same stilted fashion of the show's animation techniques.

Goodson-Toddson Reactive Narcolepsy Over-dependency on the action of game shows creating a tendency to nod off during any perceived lapse of excitement.

Test Your Teletherapy Knowledge

If you are unsure of the depth of your television knowledge, there are many instruments of evaluation. One of the most common is the Teletherapy T.I.I. (Television Intuition Index). This questionnaire of six thousand items assesses your understanding of television characters by seeking information about them never revealed on any episode of their program. Below is a sample from this extensive survey from the "Diet and Cuisine" subsection.[9] Test your intuitive knowledge of these characters:

[8] Named after Michael Ryan whose son Sean's fungus was so severe his skin had a permanent green hue.

[9] Television Intuition Index, Part IV, Section 9, Nick at Nite Teletherapy Institute, W. Miller, P. Ward, eds. 1991.

1. Which lunch selection would Lisa Douglas from *Green Acres* most likely order:

   A) arugula salad

   B) pimento loaf

   C) ham salad sandwich

   (Answer: A. The most sophisticated option for this self-styled gourmand.)

2. After dinner, Jethro Bodine from *The Beverly Hillbillies* would most likely:

   A) audibly and unselfconsciously belch

   B) pick his teeth with a matchbook cover

   C) clean his mouth with his sleeve

   D) all of the above

   (Answer: C. Granny would never tolerate the belching, and Jethro doesn't smoke and would not have a matchbook.)

3. On a visit to the city ("Mount Pilot"), which restaurant chain would Barney Fife most likely choose for a quiet supper:

   A) Roy Rogers

   B) the Olive Garden

   C) the Cracker Barrel

   (Answer: C. He would choose fast food for lunch and seek home cooking for supper. He would always avoid spicy "Eye-talion" food.)

4. While shopping for groceries to prepare for a roadside cookout for fellow members of *The A-Team,* which item would least likely be found in the grocery cart:

   A) asparagus

   B) Hamburger Helper

   C) Ring Ding Juniors

   (Answer: A. Light vegetables are the least valued sustenance for their active daily regimen.)

5. Which character used the most antacid tablets:

   A) Felix Unger

   B) Rob Petrie

   C) Archie Bunker

   (Answer: C. Felix would seek a prescription medicine, and Rob was less emotionally constricted than Archie.)

Sigmund Freud: The Father of Teletherapy

As controversial as his ideas remain, Sigmund Freud certainly developed a provocative and profound theory of human nature. While the validity of psychoanalytic technique is ever under critical scrutiny, its theoretical foundations about unconscious life are as persuasive as ever. Psychoanalysis has opened the door for people to experience relief from psychological trauma. And Teletherapy is rooted in Freudian theory.

But no one theory is complete, and even Freud knew this. Any explanation of human motivation and behavior must be highly relevant to the reality of people's lives. In Freud's day, there was no easy vehicle for communicating social and cultural norms. Customs were spread by personal contact, example, word of mouth, and ongoing personal observation. Rumors persist that to the very end of his life he remained frustrated by a key missing link in his theory. He was once quoted as telling his daughter Anna, "it's got to be there, Dear One, but I fear it remains many years off!" He was referring, of course, to television.

Had Freud lived to be 125 years old, we would all have benefited from his observations about *The Dukes of Hazard* and *My Mother the Car,* as well as *Howdy Doody*. But alas, we are left to speculation. One thing is clear, however. There is undoubtedly a significant correlation between the theories of Freud's psychoanalysis and the beliefs of teletherapy. Let's look at the evidence. Consider the following points:

Psychoanalysis	**Teletherapy**
• Believes in the unconscious	Believes TV represents the unconscious
• Uses dreams for interpretation	Sees television as America's dream content
• Developed the Oedipal Triangle	Added TV, creating the Oedipal Quadrangle
• Uses talk-therapy to heal	Uses view-therapy to heal

Teletherapy is proud to claim Sigmund Freud's theory as the predecessor of its own work. If Freud is the "father of psychoanalysis," then he is surely the "grandfather of Teletherapy." And we are his loving grandchildren. At an early Teletherapy conference in Kansas City, the theme was "Happy Birthday Sigmund Freud." The organizer of the event, in a stroke of genius, showed a clip from the movie *Heidi* with Shirley Temple. During the famous scene in which Heidi ran up the hill into the arms of her grandfather crying out in joy "Grandfather, Grandfather!" there was not a dry eye in the audience. This is why at the Teletherapy offices in New York, there is an interactive, talking statue of Freud looking at a television in the lobby. When you pull the cigar, he launches into an explanation of psychoanalysis and Teletherapy. It concludes with his thundering admonition, "Yesterday psychoanalysis, tomorrow Teletherapy!" It's a favorite feature of the tour.

What Is Tele-Denial?

Denial is the psychological defense whereby you ignore some uncomfortable reality in order to cope. It can take many forms including laughter during tense dramas or initiating conversation during talk shows. Tele-Denial occurs when you utilize television to ignore some other reality in your life. For example, by engaging in endless hours of viewing *Rush Limbaugh,* the individual uses his obsession with politics to cope with difficulties closer to home. They are thus "Rush-ing away" from their problems. This is a form of Tele-Denial. Or, they might spend excessive amounts of time watching dance shows such as *Soul Train* or reruns of *Shindig* to deny that their financial house is collapsing.

A WORD ABOUT CONFIDENTIALITY

Consistent with its object of study, Teletherapy rejects the concept of confidentiality in its sessions. In fact, a central tenet of the discipline is that we broadcast all our findings to each other and other patients. While we do not go out of our way to inform family and friends of information disclosed in sessions, we freely share it when asked. As a result of this forward thinking policy, we have opened a window and let some air into the stuffy counseling room. In addition, we have been able to assist the police in hundreds of investigations resulting in the capture and prosecution of dozens of criminals, tax cheats, and liars. We are proud of this tradition and challenge other counseling disciplines to follow our lead. We ask you, what are they afraid of, the truth?

Let's Get Started!

So now we begin your process of healing. As you proceed in the book, pay attention, study hard, and have courage. Television can be the beacon of light you have been hoping to see in your small, dark, meaningless world. It will lead you from the basement of your existence out into the bright light of day. May God go with you!

CHAPTER 3

Television and Self-Esteem

Herman Munster or Mary Richards?

Self-Esteem: So What?

Any discussion about the impact of television must begin with the self. How has the television I watched affected me? So let's talk about you. How do you feel about yourself? It's not always an easy question to answer. And yet, how we view ourselves has more impact on how we function than any other factor. Most of life's problems can be tied directly to difficulties with self-esteem. This is evident through television. Can there be any doubt that Butthead is a young man with an injured sense of self? In contrast, Detective Hutch is someone who was obviously given messages that affirmed his inner self. Compare the quality of life of Eddie Haskell and Dick Clark. The distinction is clear.

As we walk down the path of inner healing through Teletherapy, we must first establish a baseline about your sense of self. When you look in a mirror, what do you see? Do you see a highly valued, transcendent being? Or do you see a beast, a worm, a slug? Are you *The Six Million Dollar Man*? Or are you Beavis? Are you *The Bionic Woman*? Or are you merely Thing? If you feel badly about yourself, let me say clearly: You are a fool! Snap out of it! You are making your situation worse.

The fact is, and I can say this without even knowing you personally, that you are, in all probability, great! The fact that you chose this book, with its promise for renewal, means you have superior inner strength. I know that as a human being you are a grand, soul-filled eternal being. My friend, you are touched by an angel!

Before you accuse me of naiveté, of ignoring the well-documented human penchant for great evil, let me say you are wrong. I am aware that people can behave badly. If it were not so, there would be no need for Kung Fu, where even gentle priests must learn to break the bones of blockheads, boobs, and bigots. But our concern here is what lies beneath bad behaviors. Every human being was designed and destined for loving gentility and courage in interpersonal encounter. Whether you identify with Joe Mannix, or those whom he chases over the cliff in his car, at birth both Joe and the felon had the same tools for greatness.

Whatever path you have chosen, if it has been littered with broken glass, old cans, and other debris, it is most likely the result of your early life experiences, the competence of your parents, and the television influences that have shaped you. Be honest with yourself, if your life is a mess, you cannot change your childhood or your parents. But you can change your television habits. It starts with the admission that you have been a poor viewer. Say it out loud to your inner child. Look in the mirror and say, "I have been a poor viewer. I am deeply sorry! But I promise that I will take care of you from now on. I will watch television more effectively! So help me . . ."

Even if you're an individual who has repeatedly failed in life, Teletherapy can change you forever. If you are already a productive citizen, use this book to take your sense of self into an exciting new dimension. Either way, you cannot lose.

Self-Esteem Analysis

Want to measure and change your self-esteem in less than thirty days? Use this instrument developed at the Nick at Nite Self-Esteem Institute in Wayne, New Jersey. We call it "TVSET" (Transforming and Vanquishing Self-Esteem Trauma). It is guaranteed to fundamentally alter your self-perception.

1. Your true sense of self is most evident when under stress. Therefore a controlled sense of stress must be created. Close your eyes and make a tight fist so that your skin begins to turn pink. Breathe like a rabbit, in quick, short bursts. Keep this up until just before you begin to hyperventilate. With your adrenaline now flowing and your mind racing, you are prepared for accelerated insight.

2. Think about a television character who you feel most closely resembles your own personality. Bring that person's face into mind and try to see them. Who is there? What are his characteristics? Is he warm and kind, or cruel and aloof? Powerful or weak? In your mind make a list of his traits. The person who appears in your mind's eye is like an X ray, even a color snapshot, of your self-perception, telling you how you feel about yourself. This is the person you think you are and who you believe others take you to be. Let the reality, perhaps the horror, sink in fully.

3. Next, bring to mind the character you would prefer to be. Take your time and try to see their face. Now, using the tremendous power of the mind, CHANGE THE CHANNEL! You have now switched to a new program; you have become a whole new character. You are different. For example, where you once saw yourself as Uncle Fester, you have now become Keith Partridge!

4. Repeat this exercise as often as necessary.[1]

Imagine how excited you will be when, in just thirty days, your friends notice that you have an entirely new level of confidence!

---

[1] Don't be discouraged if the exercise must be repeated with great frequency. Nick at Nite Teletherapists estimate it usually takes over 300 repetitions before a new self-perception begins to take hold.

TV and Self-Esteem: Who's Who?

Okay, now that we have reoriented your sense of self, we continue. In order to establish a basis for the emerging science of Teletherapy, we must talk about the hidden meanings of some classic shows and the basic psychological health of their famous characters. It might surprise you to learn which characters were psychologically balanced and which were at risk for mental disorders. For example, which of these two classic characters do you think had better self-esteem: Herman Munster or Mary Richards?

If you said Herman Munster, excellent! Does this surprise you? It should not. Herman is the better adjusted of the two. After all, here is a severely, cosmetically challenged man, deemed hideous in appearance by almost any standard criteria of

beauty in America. Everywhere he goes he is met with reactions of revulsion to outright terror. Small children flee from his presence. And yet, Herman felt great about himself as a person. How can this be? Is he in severe denial? Perhaps. I believe Herman was aware of the reactions of people around him, but he saw it as their problem, not his. Despite his frequent frustrations with life's circumstances, Herman knew he had value as a person.

In contrast, Mary Richards, while seen as beautiful, effervescent, and highly attractive by all who met her, feels quite poorly about her core value as an individual. She is constantly struggling to feel positively about herself. In constant need of encouragement from others, she has an instinct to put the other above herself in almost every instance. It is very helpful to Mary that she is confronted daily with Ted Baxter, a regressed, marginally functional man with a narcissistic personality. By seeing Ted, she is

reminded that her own self, so routinely under attack by her negative inner voices, must have some worth after all. But she remains unconvinced.

It is not surprising that Mary cannot seem to fulfill her greatest desire for a permanent, long-term relationship in marriage. By remaining isolated from an intimate relationship (in sharp contrast to Herman, it should be noted), she betrays her chronic struggle with self-doubt. If there was only one therapist available with one open appointment, my recommendation would be for Mary to take it ahead of Herman.

Self Self-Esteem Rating

Rate the self-esteem of the following characters (remember, you are judging their *self*-worth, not your opinion of their value!).

Character	Positive Self-Esteem	Negative Self-Esteem
1. Samantha		
2. Rob Petrie		
3. Bart Simpson		
4. Flipper		

Okay, pencils down! Let's see how you did.

1. *Samantha Stephens* If you said positive self-esteem, you are right! Despite the complications of her life as a witch among mortals, Samantha has a strong sense of her self-worth. In contrast to her husband Darrin, who is riddled with self-doubt, Sam addresses life's challenges from a strong sense of her own witchly identity. The central question here is why would Samantha marry someone like Darrin, a cloying dolt? It must have been evident to her before their marriage that he was clearly uncomfortable with her extra-ordinary power. It certainly raises a question about Samantha. Why would she limit herself by marrying someone who refuses to allow her to be her true self? Could it be that she needed to marry someone she could manipulate? Certainly Darrin is no match for Sam. Someone stronger might have complicated her life even further. Regardless, Samantha is a woman of prodigious self-esteem.

2. *Rob Petrie* Sadly, Rob is struggling with his self-esteem. The very fact that he trips over the ottoman on the way into his home betrays a discomfort about himself. Who placed the ottoman there? Was it Laura, unconsciously angry at Rob's devotion to work? Might it have been his son Richie, also wanting more attention from his Dad? Or is it possible Rob is really tripping himself? Why would he do this, you ask? The answer is that he feels guilty because he is so much more emotionally connected to his job and coworkers than to his wife and family. Rob's identity is squarely rooted in his creative life at the job at the Alan Brady show. This does not mean he doesn't love Laura and Richie. It just means that, despite what he thinks he ought to feel, he cannot deny that he experiences a more profound satisfaction at work than at home. He is the type who feels edgy as the weekend drags along. Sunday nights are a delight as he eagerly anticipates his return to the job, his source of joy and gratification. Can you relate to this? Are you so bonded to work you are "tripping up" in your responsibilities at home?

"The Simpsons"™ and © 1996
Twentieth Century Fox Film Corporation.
All Rights Reserved.

3. Bart Simpson Because he is a young boy, it is not certain what the final answer is to Bart's self-esteem. He is off to a somewhat decent start, but he still has a long way to go. Like most youngsters, Bart is full of self and the bravado of prepubescent narcissism. This is what propels most adults to want to discipline him. In fact, all Bart is can be described as a raging self. With parents like his, especially a father as peppered by self-doubt and repressed rage as Homer, Bart will have to rely on the vacuous gentility of his more loving mother. It is Marge who has given Bart whatever chance he has for a strong adult sense of himself. Ideally, Bart's chances would improve if Dad would enter long-term psychotherapy, but there are no indications he will. So while the answer is positive for Bart, it is a qualified answer.

4. Flipper There are many layers of psychological meaning to Flipper. For this discussion, this remarkable creature is in fact a powerful symbol for idealized self-esteem. The key to a strong sense of self is that you can face life's challenges without succumbing to the anxiety rooted in self-doubt. Flipper can overturn a boat and its dangerous criminal without hesitation or emotional over-reaction. He sees the task ahead, instinctively assesses his capacity for accomplishing the task, and proceeds without fanfare to tackle the problem. Flipper can be a powerful teaching model for our own lives. As for the meaning of his species, remember, sometimes a bottlenose is just a bottlenose.

In summary, it is important to remember that self-confidence should not be confused with self-esteem. In fact, many people whose personalities are confident, assertive, even aggressive, are in fact struggling with a deep sense of their personal unworthiness. Using this criteria, we can easily see that many seemingly confident television characters actually view themselves quite poorly. Can you think of some examples? How about these characters:

1. Mr. Spacely—Classic Napoleon complex of a height-challenged, insecure man.
2. Archie Bunker—His angry fumings betray his fear of losing control.
3. Beavis—Adolescent, antisocial behavior is usually a mask for rage and fear about parental abandonment.
4. Alex Keaton—His inappropriate mimicry of starchy adult behavior covers his anger about the ending of maternal nurturing.
5. Sgt. Carter—The military provides a good cover for spewing his rage at unmet needs. Is he screaming at Pyle or perhaps at himself?
6. Al Bundy—Sarcasm can be a good psychological strategy to overcome feelings of being trapped and disappointed.
7. JR Ewing—What a childish fantasy! I can repay my parents for their failings by controlling and manipulating the world with the power of money right from inside their own home!

If you do not attend to the task of improving your self-esteem, you will not have as happy a life as you deserve. If you neglect your sense of self, you could begin to tailspin. Left unchecked, you could continue a downward spiral without end. At its extreme, you will soon lose your capacity to function as an independent adult. You might be institutionalized. Before you know it, you will be watching your favorite television shows on a set mounted high on a wall in a day room. In the words of Kahlil Gibran, ". . . think . . . about . . . it . . . !"

Here's a helpful exercise: Identify a character on television who appears to be self-confident but who you suspect has low self-esteem. Sit down and write him a letter telling him how you feel about his positive contributions to the other characters on his show. For example, suppose you are a *Starsky and Hutch* fan, and in your heart you feel that Starsky is struggling with some inner needs. You might want to write something like this:

Dear Starsky,

I can see right through you! You might act tough, rough, and ready for action, but I realize that behind that exterior is a little boy wanting to be loved. I have been thinking a lot about you recently. As I watch you, I can feel your frustrations about the fools you must suffer. Again and again I see you acting out in pain and anger. And I sense your terror at the thought of losing Hutch. But Starsky, my friend, you have sooo much to offer all by yourself! You don't need anyone else to make you complete. You are sooo much better than so many others....

You get the idea. It might sound silly, until it dawns on you that you are really writing to yourself, about yourself! Are you masking your inner fears and pain? Do you also believe that you too are really "sooo much better than others?" Think about it every time you see your favorite show. Think about it every day.

Your Self Is at Stake

It should be obvious to you now that Teletherapy can tackle the most daunting of all human challenges—changing your self. Many of you might be wondering if this is worth the effort. Even those of you who readily admit to having irritating qualities might be hesitant to disturb the fundamental characteristics of your personality. This is understandable. If you are unsure whether you should undertake the task of using television to change your self-image, it is recommended that you pursue an intensive investigation into the issue.

Call a meeting of your family and friends. Begin the session by telling them that you are considering changing your self-image and even your entire personality through an intensive Teletherapy program. Without further comment, evaluate their reactions. If more than half of those in attendance respond with audible approval, or even by smiling broadly, you have your answer. If more than three people use an expression such as "thank God" or "it's about time" or "finally!" it should be apparent that the treatment should begin as soon as possible. Remember, these are people in close relationship with you; you can trust their feedback.

WHERE ARE THEY NOW?

In a joint research grant shared by the Nick at Nite and Bell Laboratories, an extensive study was conducted to determine what is called the "life probability" of television characters. Using the exacting insight of Teletherapy, the scientists were able to look into the future and project, with startling accuracy, the future fate of every character that ever appeared on television. Below are the first famous characters with the results of their LPB (Life Probability Analysis), including their MLS (Mid-Life Snapshot).

Clarence "Lumpy" Rutherford This young man was clearly headed for trouble. Even as we last saw him as a friend and high school chum of Wally Cleaver, there were signs of budding personality problems. There is evidence of an eating disorder, mild antisocial behavior (such as lying and cheating), and growing anger with his parents, especially his father. Lumpy's LPB indicates a strong likelihood of underachievement and difficulty with authority.

MLS: Lumpy is a divorced father of three teenage children, all of whom are struggling in school with achievement and behavior problems. He is an insurance adjuster who has changed firms six times due to personality conflicts with his immediate supervisors. Still known as "Lumpy," he is seventy pounds overweight, drinks heavily on weekends, and has become such a devotee of football that he frequently appears at games without a shirt and with his face and body painted the team colors. He has been arrested three times for minor offenses.

CHAPTER 4

Television and Codependence

Lassie's
Disturbed Unconscious

What Is Codependence?

Codependence is a psychological illness of the self, which can be triggered by inappropriate television viewing. The numbing effect of mindless, uncritical television watching can reinforce unconscious impulses, which leads to codependent behavior. The reason is that television often creates images of idealized lifestyles. These images include vivid depictions of people who have better personalities than you, are more physically attractive than you, wealthier than you, and happier than you. This can induce self-loathing in some people.

Look at the individuals on *Baywatch*. Now look at yourself in the mirror and consider your own life. Let's be honest, yours pales in comparison. You are not as beautiful, endowed, or blessed as they are in any way, and—this is key—you have no hope of ever achieving these assets in this life. Ever. For some people, this thought becomes so depressing that it compels them to punish themselves. It raises thoughts of personal unworthiness. It engenders the idea that you are worthless refuse fit only to serve those around you in a self-emptying manner.

This feeling of unworthiness is the sum and substance of codependence. You become a servant to everyone around you. Their needs are important, yours are not. This is the twisted thinking of the codependent. What is terrifying is that some studies estimate that the incidence of codependence in America is 80 percent of the adult population. And no wonder, there is a television in virtually every home, and *Baywatch* is the "most widely viewed program in the world."[1]

If caretaking is an essential ingredient of codependency, does this mean that Alice, the Brady's housekeeper, is codependent? Not necessarily. What about the

[1] David Hasselhoff in a letter to Benny Hill, February 1991.

Nanny? Not likely. Codependency is taking care of others in order to feel good about ourselves; it is caretaking in an unhealthy way. With this in mind, it is probable that Mrs. Baxter is more codependent than her maid, Hazel. A codependent is in a psychological prison. The role one plays in society does not always indicate the illness. Sometimes it is easy to spot a codependent. Even a child with limited intellect and poor grades would say that Olive Oyl was in the advanced stages of the disease. Everyone knows Col. Henry Blake's codependence was quite progressed. Other famous television codependents include Mary Richards, Barnaby Jones, Lassie, the Skipper, and Oscar Madison.

Teletherapy's Eight Signs of Codependency

1. A persistent sense of humiliation while watching television.
2. Feelings of rage toward Marcia Brady.
3. Strong suspicion that many of the jokes on *Friends* are targeted at you and your ilk.
4. Experiencing odor memory of an unpleasant early trauma while viewing *Mister Ed*.
5. Deep desire to personally intervene while watching *Mary Tyler Moore*.
6. Nausea during *The Incredible Hulk*.
7. Powerful, lingering connection to the characters on *Cheers*.
8. You have been in a close personal relationship with at least four people who were later sent to prison.[2]

Lassie: Saintly Martyr or Severe Codependent?

Isn't it amazing that during her forty-two-year career, neither Lassie nor anyone in the family have been killed or even critically injured? According to a study into physical injuries on television at the Nick at Nite Viewing Labs in San Juan, Puerto Rico, Lassie has been involved in over nine thousand life-threatening events. What

---

[2] The criminal activity must be television-related.

is most astonishing, Lassie never backed down from one altercation, not even when fighting with snakes, mountain lions, and wild dogs. Lassie has jumped into pits, raging rivers, and mine shafts, without ever taking appropriate safety precautions. Imagine running into a forest fire without first wetting down your flowing hair! Crazy!

Is this superior courage indicative of heroic self-sacrifice or a suicidal impulse? Was Lassie an evolved spiritual being? Or was Lassie trying to find a way out of an internally tortured life? With our limited capacity to communicate with this remarkable animal, we can never know for sure. However, at the Nick at Nite Television Veterinary Labs in Richmond, Virginia, cross-species communicators have made enough progress through bark and growl analysis to believe that Lassie has an adjustment disorder, struggles with irritated bowl syndrome and bed wetting, and is depressed. Some experts speculate that Lassie, who was raised on a farm, was physically abused as a puppy by a sociopath rooster. We can only guess at the implications of this cross-species trauma. The bottom line is that we are more than a little suspicious of Lassie's emotional well-being. Researchers at the Nick at Nite Labs are persuaded that Lassie's heroics are an outgrowth of her emotional pain.

Lassie's Need to Fix

It should not surprise anyone that Lassie is severely codependent when you consider that he was the most famous cross-dresser in the history of the medium. Yes, that's right, I said "he!" Lassie, a male dog, masqueraded as a female throughout his career. Unlike Corporal Klinger, who everyone knew was pulling a scam (although there are issues here as well), Lassie was compelled to hide his gender identity in all phases of his life. Imagine the humiliation for his sons who were then told that they, too, would be forced to cross-dress just like their father? The psychological impact is staggering!

It is hard for us to empathize across species and understand the suffering in the life of a codependent dog. But imagine Lassie's relationships with his peers. Never allowed out as a male, he was utterly dependent on his human owners. His job was to perform at their beck and call, to serve others around him at all times. He was perpetually working, serving the needs of others. It is almost insultingly ironic that his human "handlers" are often referred to as Lassie's "caretakers." Ha! It isn't lost on anyone that Lassie was the ultimate caretaker!

From now on, watch Lassie with new eyes. I defy you not to weep at the sight of this pathetic little creature.

Tough Love

One accepted methodology for breaking the cycle of codependence is to engage in "tough love." This is a process in which you hold everyone in your life with a new measure of contempt and demand that they be accountable for all their negative actions toward you. It says a resounding "NO!" to any and all attempts by others to use you as their personal punching bag. It is the rejection of your doormat status. It means putting the entire family on notice that a new day has dawned. It would be like tuning in to *Leave It to Beaver* and hearing June Cleaver shout at Ward and the boys, "The party is over, Bozos! As of today, I am no longer your maid! You will do your own laundry, wash your own dishes, and clean up after yourselves. In two weeks, I am starting classes at DeVry Business School. And all of you will just like it!" As she stalks out of the room, she backhands Eddie Haskell. June is kicking butt and taking names!

Sound impossible? It is not. Difficult, yes, but not impossible. With the proper support group, and the techniques of Teletherapy, even enablers like June Cleaver and Donna Reed could smash through the cycle of codependence. With June's tough love, after an initial period of shock, Ward, Wally, and Beaver would have matured in dramatic ways. For codependents, it seems an almost insurmountable task. After years of allowing others to use and abuse them, codependents find it extremely difficult and even painful to stand up for themselves. But this is what must be done if they are to achieve the quality of life they deserve. And television can help.

Quick Teletherapeutic Codependent Exercise

Videotape two episodes of *All in the Family* for review. Whenever Archie makes a negative or cruel remark toward Edith, freeze the action and respond to Archie in the most aggressive manner possible, using your own words. For example, as soon as you hear Archie call Edith a "dingbat," freeze the tape and begin screaming back at Archie. Really let him have it, remarking on his weight, his low IQ, his paltry salary, and chronic relationship difficulties.

As soon as you have finished, turn off the tape and begin another, unrelated activity. DO NOT WATCH the conclusion of the scene. This could potentially undo the positive effects of the exercise. The idea is to not allow the abuser, Archie, the last word. Soon this sequence will become habit in your real life. When someone behaves hurtfully toward you, your response will be swift and punishing. Before long, both you and your family will learn a new rhythm of behaving. Others will be put on notice that they abuse you at their own peril.

Finding a New Resolve

One way to determine if you are a codependent is if, right now, you are perspiring. This means that the material in this chapter is hitting a nerve of recognition, and you are feeling threatened by it. Very likely your mind is racing frantically trying to find a way to please me right now. If you are perspiring but do not feel a need to serve me, this is your denial. Either way, your discomfort is betraying your codependence.

Once codependence is diagnosed, the first feeling most enablers experience is a sense of doom and despair; they cannot find the resolve to stand up for themselves. The martyrdom instinct is so deeply woven into the psyche that changing it appears to be an insurmountable task. Where can we find the strength to stop this self-flagellation? The answer is right there in your den: the television. Television can give you what you cannot give yourself. Think about the fantastic dual characteristic of the TV. On the one hand, it is a completely passive implement that you can control! You decide when to turn it on and when to turn it off. You decide when to stay with a program and when to change channels. You hold the power! Yet on the other hand, the television is replete with assertive messages. The content is bold and frequently aggressive. It is filled with teaching images, which confront your codependence, and beckons you twenty-four hours a day to stand up for yourself and get happy!

These twin characteristics of television mean that it can be used to both confront and change you. It snaps the rigid rod of denial, which impedes your emotional mobility, while it simultaneously empowers you as an individual. But finding the strength to take charge of your life must begin with small, baby steps. No codependent gets cured overnight. With conventional treatment, it usually takes years. Even with Teletherapy's inpatient treatment, most codependents take a week to fully recover. A self-directed home study Teletherapy course will take up to thirty days.[3] But as Freud himself stated, "the important thing is to start."[4]

[3] There were two documented cases of complete cures instantly while watching *Roseanne* and *Grace Under Fire* episodes. In separate instances, the two began watching as severe codependents and were totally cured by the end of the show. But this is rare and should not serve as a model.

[4] Although the context for this statement had to do with rowing in his son's canoe, it has been surmised that he was actually talking about psychological treatment.

Assertiveness Through Television

Start with this humble strategy for learning to seize control of your life through the following progressive exercise:

1. Stand up in front of your television with a remote control in your hand. Turn to C-Span or some other low energy station (The Weather Channel is not recommended during twister or tropical storm season).
2. Practice turning the set off and on according to your own inner decision, not related to the content of the show. State your intentions out loud in a commanding tone of voice, "I turn you off!" and then "I turn you on!"
3. When you feel greater confidence, switch to a more intense channel, such as The Cartoon Network or MTV, and try it again. Work your way up so that you are able to even watch your favorite channel and turn it off right in the middle of the episode!
4. As you become advanced in this technique, set a timer for a random amount of time and use it as a signal to quick draw the remote and turn off the television.

Teletherapy: Foundation of Recovery

Although we will address the issue of complete recovery from all television-based illnesses in a later chapter, we can state categorically that Teletherapy cures codependence in all its insidious forms. When patients arrive for an in-patient stay at the Nick at Nite Recovery Clinic in New Paltz, New York, they are immediately placed on a program of selected television viewing designed to break through their denial. Using sophisticated software, the staff has created the ability to superimpose the faces of the patients and their significant others onto the cast of certain television shows. As they sit in their isolation booth and watch, the patients see themselves and their family on the screen in an episode of *Cheers,* for example. Through a carefully designed lineup of shows, the patients become Edith Bunker, Rob Petrie, Aunt Bea, and Mr. Greenjeans. This allows them to see themselves and their loved ones in various roles as codependent, addictive, or allegedly healthy.

The sequence of this experience takes them from deeply codependent characters through increasingly healthy models. It concludes when the patients see themselves in several characters who represent less codependent individuals. For example, they might see themselves as Roseanne Connor, screaming in righteous rage at a noxious boss who has a history of verbally abusing people. Or they might see themselves as Heckle, the aggressive crow who, along with his sibling Jeckle, consistently rebuff all attempts to victimize them.

Upon returning home, the patient is encouraged to dress and behave like one of these healthier models for the first several weeks. Support is the key.

Organized Teletherapy 12-Step Support Groups are an ongoing part of the recovery process. If there is no listing in the phone directory for a Teletherapy Support Group, start one yourself. Failure to do so would indicate an unhealthy pattern of immobility. In fact, if three weeks from now,

53

you have still not taken the initiative to start a Teletherapy Support Group, this might well be a sign that your codependence is quite advanced and inpatient treatment is recommended. Contact your physician and advise him of your concern.

WHERE ARE THEY NOW?

Below is another famous character with the results of their LPB (Life Probability Analysis), including their MLS (Mid-Life Snapshot). See chapter 3 for more details.

Pugsley Addams: It is hard to fathom the impact of an entire childhood at odds with your peers. While many people can relate to a childhood filled with the sting of ostracism, nothing could compare to what the Addams boy endured. But in many ways this became his principle resource. Pugsley had to find his strength from the strong affirmation of his parents and within himself. The financial resources and unstinting love of Gomez and Morticia, and the mentoring of his Uncle Fester, created a fertile environment for growth. Pugsley's LPB shows a solid line of academic achievement in the sciences, but with a twist.

MLS: Pugsley has become a noted and respected engineer at the Microsoft laboratories. He has designed several significant computer software systems that are in wide use. A visit to his home, however, attests to his family penchant for the weird edges of life. He has several exotic pets, eats only uncooked, organic foods, and collects both stamps and the skins of road kill. At the age of forty-two, he marries a gentle, but troubled actuary with a history of chronic psychotic breaks. They leave the city and raise Shetland ponies on a small farm in New Mexico.

CHAPTER 5

Television and Dysfunction

We Are All Jethro!

How Dysfunctional Are You?

In general, there are two overarching categories of individuals accepted by most mental health practitioners and their professional organizations, including the Nick at Nite Psychiatric Consortium in Steamboat Springs, Colorado. These two categories are "normal" and "abnormal." To ascertain into which category you fall, there are several television-based assessment tools that can serve as guides. One of these, for example, is called "Teletherapae Extremis" (Teletherapy in Extreme Situations). It scans your television preferences while you are in a perilous or horrifying situation. The results can offer significant insight. It's a quick test of your symptoms of dysfunction.

Answer the following three questions:

1. Imagine you are in an appliance store being held at gunpoint in a hostage situation. As you wait for the negotiations to conclude, which reality based show would most help relax you:

   a) *Crossfire*
   b) *The Jerry Springer Show*
   c) *Studs*

Functional Choice: *Studs* (The key to relaxing is to divert your attention away from your imminent death.)

Dysfunctional Choices: *Crossfire* (indicates hyperawareness of severely dysfunctional behavior patterns); Jerry Springer (could indicate codependent, self-defeating compassion for the perpetrator)

2. Imagine you are fleeing from a disgruntled coworker and have run into a videostore to escape. As you are lying flat on the carpet hoping the maniac will pass by outside, you see three videotapes are in view. Which of these films based on a television show would remind you of a life-sustaining strategy:

    a) *The Beverly Hillbillies*
    b) *The Brady Bunch*
    c) *The Addams Family*

Functional Choice: *The Addams Family* (indicates an acceptance of death and thus a freedom to think with less fear)

Dysfunctional Choices: *The Beverly Hillbillies* (could lead you to think that life, even with money, is not worth living and deflate your will to live); *The Brady Bunch* (could make you think about your own, less ideal family and deflate your will to live)

3. Imagine you are in a severe windstorm. Your vehicle has overturned and you are trapped inside. The vehicle is slowly sliding into a river with vicious white-water turbulence. Which of the following television animals would you most like to arrive to help:

    a) *Mister Ed*
    b) *Rin Tin Tin*
    c) *Arnold Ziffel*

Functional Choice: Mister Ed (Although probably not personally motivated to assist you, he could be coaxed into kicking in a window for a French fry found on your car floor. And Ed is the best equipped to remove the window.)

Dysfunctional Choices: Rin Tin Tin (Since you are a civilian and a stranger to him, precious moments could be lost as he ascertains whether you are a criminal.); Arnold Ziffel (has limited history of life-saving skills or motivation to assist in human crises)

If you answered one question incorrectly, you should consider yourself diagnosed as a dysfunctional person. If you answered two questions incorrectly, you should seek professional counseling. If you answered all three questions incorrectly, immediate hospitalization is recommended. If, on the other hand, you answered all three questions correctly, further testing is in order.

Teletherapy's Ten Core Symptoms of Personal Dysfunction

1. Drowsiness during *Baywatch*.
2. Consistently irritated by Mr. Rogers.
3. Engaging in a total immersion experience at a *Star Trek* convention.
4. Needing to see which character is wearing a uniform to determine who is the hero in *True Stories of the Highway Patrol*.
5. Difficulty in defining the precise moment of transition from a program to a commercial.
6. Persistently siding with Louis DePalma in matters of choice.
7. Seeing Judge Wapner as a role model.
8. Experiencing fear during *Hee Haw*.
9. Free-floating inertia.
10. Selection as an alien abductee and surgical victim.

The A-Team and Television's Role in Creating Dysfunction

Despite protestations to the contrary, television is far and away the leading shaper of group values and norms. While this thought might terrify many and provoke envy in higher intellectual circles, it is not as controversial as some would believe. Some suggest that television is the cause of antisocial and aberrant behavior across the land. Teletherapy asserts that the actions of sociopaths, felons, miscreants, and malcontents are actually the result of toxic family life where television was chronically misused. The problem is usually that the real meanings of the shows were completely misunderstood in some homes.

When a young child is sitting with the family in front of the television, he is keenly observant of the modeling by his parents. If, for example, as a young child you were watching *The A-Team* with your family, you would notice that your parents seem to be rooting for the Team against the authorities. The result is that you are given a very persuasive message that fosters several key conclusions. In this particular example, you would conclude the following:

1. Jewelry equates with physical power. This can cause later feelings of intimidation when faced with anyone, male or female, wearing an abundance of jewelry.
2. There is an association between cigar smoking and leadership. This could very well be a leading cause of teenage nicotine addiction.
3. Contusions heal without scarring within forty-eight hours. This can lead to a false sense of courage in altercations.

The result of these messages from this one show alone can cultivate an adult personality with several antisocial characteristics, including inappropriate accessorizing, public cigar smoking, and frequent provocations to physical violence in routine social settings. If only your parents had shown you that the real message of the A-Team was impotence. Using the metaphor of compliant young draftees, who served their country heroically but who then are falsely accused of criminal activity, provides an example about our own struggles against sometimes obtuse authority.

If during the commercial, your father had only said, "You see, dear one, sometimes you will view Mommy and me as dull-witted and intractable as the officers who are pursuing the A-Team. But you will be able to use your resourcefulness to circumvent our authority if you choose. Just remember there are consequences that can often times be quite brutal. This is just a warning."

Dream Analysis Case File 1

The Nick at Nite Labs are inundated with letters offering testimonials about the miracle of Teletherapy. Much of this mail includes descriptions of dreams involving television characters. For a fee, the Nick at Nite scientists analyze these dreams for the patient. Here is a dream someone sent to us and Teletherapy's analysis of it.

I was walking down a long corridor with Captain Kirk from *Star Trek*. We were on our way to a court hearing where I was being charged with the crime of assaulting Blanche Devereaux from *The Golden Girls* after she made a pass at my father. We entered the courtroom, I could see that the judge was Max Headroom and the prosecuting attorney was Judge Wapner from *The People's Court*. Seeing how shocked I was at seeing Judge Wapner, Captain Kirk whispered in my ear, "Wapner was thrown off the bench for assaulting a guest on his show and he's now a prosecuting attorney." I felt a surge of rage and leaped over a table and smacked Wapner as I screamed, "in the case of the 'Mis-Clipped Poodle,' you were completely wrong, you arrogant jackass!" As two guards restrained me, everyone in the courtroom burst into applause, and Judge Headroom started laughing uncontrollably. I then woke up sweating.

—Mr. Jack Henry,
New Brunswick, New Jersey

Teletherapy's Interpretation: What is clear from this dream is that you are struggling with authority. You have a keen sense of which is legitimate authority and which is fraudulent, regardless of their position in society. For example, even though he holds a position of prestige, you perceive that Wapner is a fraud. You trust Captain Kirk with your case, but seem unsure of Max Headroom as a judge. Why and what does this mean? The key is the uniform. Having an outward sign of power is not always a trustworthy test of a person's integrity. This dream is telling you that you can trust your gut instincts about who is a legitimate authority and who is not. Congratulations!

We Are All Jethro!

One of the most flamboyantly dysfunctional characters in the history of television was Jethro Bodine, nephew of Jed Clampett of *The Beverly Hillbillies*. Here was a young man who functioned at a minimal level, showed signs of delusions, and was quite probably psychotic. And he thus becomes the symbol of our own dysfunction. *The Beverly Hillbillies* tells the story about an uneducated rural family

that becomes rich overnight. While their social skills are quite advanced within their own native culture, they make a devastating choice by relocating away from their home and kin to a wealthy show business community. As a result, each member of the family becomes psychiatrically ill in their frantic but futile efforts to adapt to their peculiar new circumstances.

Among the pathologies that flower in this most dysfunctional family are depression, adjustment disorders, substance abuse, intermittent explosive disorder and, in Jethro's case, a severe detachment from reality in a reactive psychosis. In his struggle for sanity, we learn a valuable lesson. It is quite probable that Jethro, who perhaps was intellectually limited and immature while living back home, was nonetheless a functional young member of that indigenous society. If his responsibilities included hunting for food provision, routine household chores, and actively seeking a mate for wedlock, then he was well equipped for life there. But taken out of his natural habitat, he quickly deteriorates into a fantasy world.

There is little doubt that Jethro went on to be institutionalized within three more years of life in California. The message to us is clear: Adapt to your native environment or face the perils of deterioration and sanity. You must learn to adapt or you will soon drown in your own dysfunction. Put his picture on your wall and each day remind yourself: "I am Jethro, Jethro is me!"

Teletherapy's Draw-a-Person Test

One reliable method for determining whether you are normal or abnormal is to use an example of your art work. By analyzing how you draw another individual, the scientists can ascertain your mental health.

On a clean sheet of paper, and using a crisply sharpened pencil with thick lead, draw a stick-figure picture of your father, your mother, and your oldest sister (if you do not have a sister, imagine you do and draw her). Do not use the real-life individuals as models, or even photographs. Draw from memory and your own unconscious. Draw rapidly and without thinking. Don't try to trick or out-think the scientists. It never works, and they can tell when you have tried to cheat. This will reflect badly on your score. Do not edit or revise the picture. Immediately send it to the staff at the Nick at Nite Personality Institute in Jonesboro, Tennessee. The results will be mailed to you within 7–10 weeks. Good luck!

CHAPTER 6

Television and Rage
Killing
the Gilligan Within

The Dilemma of Anger

No theory of psychological healing is valid if it fails to address anger, perhaps the most fundamental of all human struggles. Anger is the cause of untold amounts of misery and failure. It has baffled the greatest minds in history. Every great thinker has wrestled with the problem of anger; millions of great and wise words have been expressed to help us in the battle against our inner rage. Freud himself admitted that trying to adequately define the concept of anger was a task that often enraged him.[1] My own father said to me when I was ten years old, "don't be angry . . . ever." Moving in its simplicity, these words served as a guiding force as I entered the field of mental health and sought to unravel the mystery of this most disquieting human emotion. After many years of intense study, many of which enraged me as well, imagine my euphoria when it suddenly struck me that television was the answer!

There can be no doubt that we are in desperate need of a new response to human anger. Many strategies have been developed, all to little effect. The fact is that American society has become a boiling cauldron of contempt, a percolating pot of provocation, an oven of animosity. Where can we turn for relief? What is the common denominator? As we look around for a source of hope, it becomes

---

[1] One incident involved throwing pool equipment out a window while vacationing at a spa and trying to collect his thoughts on the subject of anger.

apparent that what we all share is the reflective glow of the television screen on our hot faces. It is through television that we can be reached. This is the essence of the miracle of Teletherapy. This is what I discovered several years ago.

Television-Related Signs That You Are Struggling with Anger

Perhaps you are unaware if your anger has become a problem for you. Using your experience as a viewer, see if these signs seem familiar to you:

1. Tearing labels off beverage bottles while viewing television.
2. While channel surfing, making exaggerated changing gesture to move past religious programming.
3. Unnecessarily loud hand striking when using "The Clapper" device.
4. Habitual lip biting while watching rugby.
5. Lingering fantasies of retaliation against inconsiderate behavior by sitcom characters. For instance, spending more than twenty minutes ruminating about a confrontation with Ted Baxter. (If this behavior includes actually making a physical list of such strategies, or attempts to make contact with the actor, seek help as soon as possible.)

Eureka!

I will never forget that night in the laboratory. It was late in the night of yet another frustrating day of seemingly fruitless research. I was working with the same small community of rats. My experiments focused not on the intense rage of some major provocation, but on the more common experience of enduring the simple stupidity and clumsiness of others around us. I had conditioned one individual rat to be clumsy and physically inept. Named "Bradley," I felt pity for this little creature, often finding myself staring at him through the cage and weeping quietly. But I was resolved that the research must continue. Each time I placed Bradley in

with the other rats, he inadvertently spilled water, tripped another rat, or otherwise made life difficult for them. Each time, a remarkable thing happened. The injured rat did nothing to Bradley, but it carried its stress around for several hours. The injured rat tolerated Bradley because it knew he was not intentionally impeding him. Why?

What was the key? I knew the answer was there, so close! Distractedly, I turned on the television. A commercial was just ending and the show resumed. It was *Gilligan's Island*. The professor had just pieced together yet another makeshift radio that was receiving transmissions. I laughed because I just knew what was coming. Sure enough, Gilligan, unintentionally but inevitably, destroyed the radio. And the others did nothing! I heard myself mumble out loud, "Why, the professor would probably really like to kill him!" At that exact same moment, I heard a disturbance in the rat environment. Bradley, the dumb rat, had spilled water onto the head of another rat. As usual, the soaked rat did not attack Bradley, but simply screeched at him, just like the professor had not attacked Gilligan, but merely screamed at him! Eureka! My first impulse was to turn and shout to Bradley, "Your name is now Gilligan!"

In the flash of an instant, it all became clear. *Gilligan's Island* is about the repressed rage we feel at those inept, self-defeating fools around us. We all encounter Gilligans (or Bradleys) who trip us up in life. We, too, hold down our anger, allowing it to tear at us inside. Wow! Television had unlocked the door to a

PERSONAL REJECTION

When I first suggested on Nick at Nite that *Gilligan's Island* is actually a show about human rage, many people, including several of my colleagues, ridiculed the idea. At one professional conference, a noted psychologist, I'll call him "Dr. R.," exploded in anger at me.[2] Purple with rage, and in front of a large group of our peers, he slapped his glove across my face and shouted, "your Gilligan theory is nonsense!" Luckily the decorative button on his glove missed my lip and I was uninjured. Instead of responding in kind with violence, I collected myself and retorted, "if you say so, Skipper." The crowd gasped as they immediately caught my meaning. I had exposed his inner Skipper!

The inner Skipper is the unconscious impulse found in every one of us, which seeks to retaliate with murderous anger against the Gilligans in our life. As soon as I called him Skipper, Dr. R., brilliant thinker that he is, made the connection. Flustered and realizing what had happened, he broke down weeping. Through his tears he sobbed, "I'm so sorry, little buddy." He asked my forgiveness and, transformed, has since become a noted Teletherapist. But his was typical of the early resistance to a new theory, which later became famous as Teletherapy.

great human mystery for me. I grabbed Gilligan the rat and kissed him. He urinated in my hand and I laughed. My life turned in a new direction and Teletherapy was born!

The Gilligan Within!

It all began with that simple premise: we each have both a "Gilligan Within" and a "Skipper Within." The "Gilligan Within" is that part of us that is self-defeating, that gets in the way of other people. Have you ever been late to pick someone up and thus caused them to miss an appointment? Have you ever forgotten to do something that created a problem for someone else? Of course you have, we are all guilty of these little blunders. Whenever you make a mistake that impedes

[2] Dr. Stuart Robertson, 14 Hollow Road, Wheaton, IL (zip code withheld upon request).

another person or that causes another to lose an opportunity, your "Inner Gilligan" has risen up. Like Gilligan who, however consciously, unintentionally destroyed the lives of six other innocent people, we all have been the cause of another's missed opportunities. All of the castaways, but in particular, the Skipper, must repress the impulse to retaliate against Gilligan. Whenever you struggle with feelings of retaliation against someone whose "Inner Gilligan" has interrupted your life, it is your "Inner Skipper" rising. In the above scenario, I played Gilligan to Dr. R.'s Skipper.

You might be wondering about other television characters. At a recent introductory Teletherapy seminar, a young man asked, "But if we all have Gilligans and Skippers within ourselves, doesn't this mean that we also have other television characters inside of us as well?" This was a great question. As he was hustled from the room by security, I called back an emphatic "yes!"[3] Whatever shows you watched and absorbed as a child, those characters are living within you.

Erkel: Symbol of Repressed Rage

At a gut level, what is your reaction to the following assertion: "Erkel is the most dangerous young man on television!" Does it seem ludicrous? Preposterous? Absurd? If so, then you desperately need the teachings in this chapter. It could, quite literally, save your life! The fact is, your rejection of this statement (which, by the way, is an irrefutable truth) indicates your disconnection from crucial psychological insight not just about television, but about your entire life. Failing to understand that Erkel is dangerous, even potentially lethal, places you at personal risk for the day an Erkel in your life blows his lid. In today's world, it is imperative that you be alert to the signs of an Erkel's deterioration so that you can get out of his path.

You are puzzled. Okay, let me take a brief moment and explain the "Erkel" phenomenon. A basic principle of Teletherapy is "reaction formation." This means that a person's conscious attitudes often express the opposite of his inner, unconscious desires. When we have a wish or impulse that makes us uncomfortable, before we even bring it to our awareness, we formulate a reaction against that

---

[3] He was not ejected because of his question, but because of his refusal to stand while speaking.

wish. A classic illustration is found in what is called "anal retention" whereby excessive neatness is a reaction against an inner desire to creatively soil oneself. This is a rebellion against the mother's demand that the child use the restroom properly. The child wants to be the one who determines when to stop at the gas station and when to continue driving. By withholding creative forces, one asserts control over mother.

Now let's get back to Erkel. His dress, demeanor, and lifestyle suggest the classic "nerd." He appears to be submissive, without physical prowess, an easy target for the cruel dominance of stronger, more aggressive peers. His presentation of himself leads us to suspect that he is in "reaction formation" against his inner impulses to uncork his deep rage. The degree to which Erkel is the meek nerd, is the same degree to which he has an inner desire to lash out and kill! Heaven help those in his path when he snaps! His fury will be boundless.

In the meantime, Erkel, like all nerds, will continue to express his repressed rage in passive ways. Support for this theory is found in the story line where Erkel invents a machine that changes him into "Stefan," his ultracool alter ego. This vivid hallucination is Erkel's wish to be other than he is, but cannot tolerate becoming. He prefers to remain the nerd, repressing his wrath.

In real-life, practical terms, this is known as "passive-aggressive" anger. We see this behavior every day. It is displayed by the person driving forty miles an hour in the left lane of the interstate. It is displayed in the supermarket when someone takes twenty items through the express line. It is displayed whenever someone is being infuriatingly slow or obstructive. Their outer behavior says passive, but their inner motivation is rage!

Incredible Hulk: Universal Symbol of Repressed Rage

Teletherapy takes the position that every human being struggles with inner impulses of murderous aggression. We all experience moments of deep anger, which sometimes come to the surface and are acted out or sometimes repressed and bottled up inside. The trick is to live out a balance of appropriate expression and healthy repression. We cannot act on every angry impulse or we would soon be in prison along with others who struggle with control problems. But equally destructive is repressing too much of our anger. This can lead to serious psychological problems including depression, poor job performance, ulcers, and general free-floating malaise.

Thus the key question becomes: How can I discharge these feelings in a way that will not hurt myself or those I love? In addressing this daunting human challenge, TV offered us *The Incredible Hulk*. The Hulk is the other identity alive within Dr. David Banner. The Hulk is the embodiment of David's inner rage. It is so palpable that it has taken on an actual form. The deeper message in this show is that even if you grow up to become a successful, peaceful, functioning member of society, beware! Lurking inside you, just beneath the surface of your controlled exterior, there lies something awful, something overwhelming—an ugly green beast who tears off his own clothes!

That's right, each of us has a "Lou Ferrigno Within." To any sane person, this is a terrifying prospect. For each of us, it is a lifelong task to control this powerful inner monster, to channel these passions. Television exposes the reality of this hideous green inner beast, deaf to others, unable to speak.

Andy and Barney: Two Decisive Strategies for Rage

The classic television program *The Andy Griffith Show* was a textbook illustration of the dynamics of human anger. It offers two distinct models, Andy Taylor and Barney Fife, for responding to the inner impulses of human anger. As you read these descriptions, assess your own response. Are you more like Sheriff Taylor or Deputy Fife? The answer not only tells you a great deal about yourself, it also becomes the starting place for your own healing.

First, however, let's consider the setting of the show. The town of Mayberry is in North Carolina, and the name is a significant clue. Seen as a two-word phrase, it

sounds like and becomes "may bury," as in "something may bury you." What is the meaning of this illusion? Clearly it refers to the different approaches to life pursued by the two lead characters. So let's look at them now.

Andy Taylor: Pacifist Hero

The hero in the show is clearly Sheriff Andy Taylor, a widowed father who served as the sheriff of this little home town. His style is easygoing, even tempered, and peace loving. Even as a lawman, Andy always seeks a nonviolent solution to all problems. Regardless of how belligerent a criminal might be, his style is to use reason and good will to resolve the crisis. He does not carry a gun in what is a radical statement about his priorities. In essence, Andy represents the model of calm and healthy repression of inner rage impulses.

Barney Fife: Edgy Cop

In vivid contrast to his supervisor is the style of Deputy Barney Fife. He is nervous, perpetually agitated, and easily provoked. He not only carries a weapon, he is quick to brandish it. There is little doubt that Barney would be willing to pull the trigger long before Andy. His anger is percolating and palpable. Left unchecked, it is very likely that Barney would become engaged in physical altercations on a routine basis as part of his work. There is little doubt, for instance, that Barney would very likely beat Otis, the alcoholic, on a consistent basis with his fists or some professional law enforcement implement. Barney represents the model of unbridled, expressive anger with minimal repression of his inner rage impulses.

The preference for Andy's method of responding to his inner anger is made clear in both the emotional style and physical appearance of the two men. On the one hand, Andy is warm, kind, and evidently at peace with himself. He is also a robust and physically healthy individual. By comparison, Barney is fidgety, panicky, and ill at ease with all but the most benign strangers. His physical appearance suggests an eating disorder or, more likely, irritable bowel syndrome as a result of his excitable, neurotic inner conflict.

In treating these two, Andy might have to work on unresolved issues of grief over the loss of his wife, and Barney would very likely be medicated. Imagine the renewed Barney on Prozac. He has gained forty pounds, he is visibly calmer and more pleasant to be around. As a result, even the troublesome members of the

community would approach him with greater respect. He would have gained the resources to contain his eruptive anger and calmed his digestive system at the same time.

There is no doubt that *The Andy Griffith Show* is a convincing allegory for balanced repression of human anger in contrast to the evident futility of allowing it to rise up too easily. All the other characters in the show serve as foils for this fundamental lesson. All are either uncomplicated innocents or impotent simpletons. The benevolence of the rural surroundings accentuates that this is not a place where you can expect to have your anger provoked by any antagonistic behavior. This is a place where Goober Pyle and Floyd Lawson safely walk the streets. This only serves to accentuate the purity of the anger issue. It is never provoked in Mayberry. And now we answer the question about that name. The answer is that Barney's style of unrepressed anger may bury him before his time. Teletherapy asks you the same question: Are you in denial about your anger? Do you know which television shows caused this condition? Are your current viewing choices threatening to bury you, too?

CHAPTER 7

Television and Depression

If Only
the Rifleman Had Prozac

New American Health Crisis:
TBD (Television-Based Depression)

If an intimidating, well-muscled stranger approached you and said, "Quick! Without thinking about it, name a famous television star who is depressed!" undoubtedly you would answer, "The Maytag Repairman." A recent survey taken by the researchers at the Nick at Nite Television Polling Institute in Baton Rouge, Louisiana, placed him at the top of the list, followed by

2. Robert Ironsides
3. Ed Sullivan
4. Bobby Ewing
5. Control's Chief

These are revealing answers, because they expose a popular misconception in the culture. Many people assume that depression is simply a severe form of sadness. This is a pathetic and damaging myth, one caused by defective television viewing habits.

Although melancholy is frequently a part of depression, the condition is a lot more complicated than simply excessive sadness. In fact, depression frequently includes a variety of symptoms, some of which appear to be anything but sad. They might also involve irritation, sleeplessness, disturbance of diet, and social withdrawal. Depression that is rooted in television viewing has several additional significant symptoms. Although these behaviors are clearly seen as odd by family and friends, their connection to television depression is rarely made.

Eight Signs a Loved One Has Television-Based Depression

Perhaps you are wondering whether you or someone you love has TBD. Here are a few signs you should easily observe. Are they familiar?

1. Viewing in a transfixed manner with the mouth always open.
2. Repeated sniffing in the air as if trying to determine an odor.
3. Channel surfing at a pace that prevents knowing station content.
4. Changing clothes at least once during a one-hour drama.
5. Profuse sweating while watching animation.
6. Taping for reviewing episodes of *Carnie*.
7. Lipsynching Dionne Warwick's dialogue on the Psychic Friends Network infomercial.
8. Inappropriate risk-taking behavior while trying to repair electronic devices.

The cause of Television-Based Depression is unknown, but there are two widely recognized, competing theories. One says that the ailment is caused when certain individuals suddenly become aware that they are not able to smell, feel, or taste the experiences their favorite shows depict. In other words, some people become so lost in the world of what they are viewing, they become unconsciously aware that they are not sharing all the experiences of the characters on the show. They feel left out, isolated, and hopeless about their disconnection. Before too long, they stop believing that they can sense the experiences of their actual, nonviewing life. They become suspicious of smells and feelings in real life. These sensory experiences feel alien and false to them.

In an experiment at the Nick at Nite Viewing Labs, victims of TBD were able to "experience" episodes of *Hogan's Heroes* using virtual reality technology, which included the dank smell of barracks, the feel of the camp's breeze on their skin, and even the sour, gum-diseased breath of Sergeant Shultz. In all but one case, and to the delight of the researchers, the symptoms of TBD lifted.[1] The patients reported a sense of well-being and a desire to reengage in social activities (in particular, line dancing).

The other theory argues that Television-Based Depression is triggered by a brain-wave abnormality associated with the voices and physical movements of very thin women, examples of which abound on television. There are strong advocates on each side of the debate. According to Dr. Elgin Fields, Director of Viewing Research, "It's either one or the other, both, or even neither."[2] Time will tell.

For now, we will allow for either possibility. Regardless of the true cause, TBD

is a difficult public health problem. Teletherapy has designed several treatments that have proven effective. Most of these can be used at home by nonprofessionals and involve materials generally found around the home. What is important is that the patient not ignore the problem. Think of it this way, if television is the window into the American psyche, then the programs are the fuel that fires the furnace. Thus depression would be like either failing to change the furnace's filter or running dangerously low on oil.[3] Think about it!

If someone you know shows some of the symptoms of TBD, and you would like to clarify whether they are television depressed, merely eccentric, or even simply crazed, there is a Teletherapeutic quick test available to you.

---

[1] The one exception was a woman who was misdiagnosed with TBD. Upon further evaluation, it turned out she was suffering the aftereffects of a lightning strike, which came through her television set inside her den. She recovered fully and is now a practicing Teletherapist in South Carolina.

[2] Speech to attendees of the third anniversary celebration of C-Span 2.

[3] A natural gas conversion metaphor is available upon request from the Natural Gas Association.

Teletherapy's TBD Quick Test

1. In preparation, videotape one episode each of *Walker, Texas Ranger* and *The Brady Bunch*.
2. Watch these episodes repeatedly until you are fully familiar with the show's content.
3. Next, arrange a time of monitored viewing with the depressed individual. Tell them that you are concerned that they might have Television-Based Depression, and you would like to try an experiment. Assure them it is quick and painless. If they consent, have them sit in front of the television.
4. As they view the shows, create multisensory experiences connected with the program content, which cannot be experienced through the television. Specifically, we are talking about smell, touch, and taste. Thus, if there is a meal being cooked and served, create these aromas in the den. If there are outdoor scenes, use a small fan to create the effect of a breeze. If it is raining, use a small spray bottle aimed toward the face. But in all of this, try to be as unintrusive as possible. The point is to create these sensory experiences as background for the show.
5. After seeing the shows through once with the multisensory assistance, ask the individual to repeat the experience once more. This time, do not provide any more sensory stimulation. Observe the person closely as they watch the second time through.
6. If the person appears generally sadder on the second viewing, more emotionally distressed in the repeat experience, you are very likely dealing with TBD. If they have no different reaction on the second viewing, this would suggest that TBD is not a factor for them. (If the person has the opposite reaction, that is, they appear happier during the second viewing, call a physician or local mental health facility immediately! The individual may very well require hospitalization.)

The Role of Medication

The miracle of modern science includes the widespread use of medications for a wide variety of human ailments. And TBD is no exception. In recent years there has been dramatic and exciting progress in the treatment of depression. By now, most people are familiar with Prozac, the wonder drug that appears to radically ease depressive symptoms with surprisingly few side effects. While some controversy persists about its safety and efficacy, there has been widespread enthusiasm for the life-changing impact this drug has had for many people.

Teletherapy is a treatment that does not include medication as part of its process. There is a simple reason for this. While many Teletherapists have extensive training in a variety of academic fields, medicine is rarely one of them. In

IF ONLY THEY HAD PROZAC

Television is filled with characters whose personality problems caused untold suffering for themselves and the others in their lives. Their mood disorders compelled them to act out in so many inappropriate ways that the people around them had to alter their lives dramatically to compensate for them. In many instances, these personality problems were the result of a neurotic depression. I would prescribe Prozac for the following:

Character	Show
Curly Howard	*The Three Stooges*
Officer Bill Gannon	*Dragnet*
Jan Brady	*The Brady Bunch*
Sister Bertrille	*The Flying Nun*
Dr. Frank Burns	*M*A*S*H*
Pugsley Addams	*The Addams Family*
Floyd the Barber	*The Andy Griffith Show*
Sgt. Nick Yamana	*Barney Miller*

other words, almost no Teletherapists are qualified to prescribe drugs. In fact, a breakdown of the core training of the profession reveals that 31 percent have a background in metaphysics, 14 percent in parapsychology, 11 percent in law, 7 percent in engineering, and the remainder in the construction trades, especially electrical and heating and cooling. This is not to say that Teletherapists are against medication. Quite the contrary. Surveys of their practice indicate that the use of prescribed medication jumps 41 percent within the first year of Teletherapy treatment.

Medication should be the treatment of last resort. Radical behavioral intervention is always the preferred option in Teletherapy. The guiding principle is always, "How can I use television to bring the cure?" But when drugs are indicated, they obviously alter the Teletherapeutic treatment for that patient. Obviously, using interventions calling for exposing the patient to extremely high TV sound volume would be unwise if they are taking pain medication for dental treatment. A trained Teletherapist understands these basic tenets.

Medication

Each of the characters below had chronic psychological problems that could have been eased with the right medication. Can you match the character with their needed medicine?

Character	Medication
Dennis Mitchell	Thorazine
Granny Clampett	Nicorette gum
Joe Friday	Ritalin
David Banner	Anabuse

Answers: Dennis—Ritalin for Attention Deficit Disorder; Granny—Anabuse for alcohol abuse; Joe—Nicorette gum for tobacco dependence; David—Thorazine for psychosis.

Television Detectives: Suicidal TBD!

Does the following assertion startle you: "Frank Cannon, Jim Rockford, and Joe Mannix were certainly murdered within twelve months of the cancellation of their shows. And I strongly suspect each one participated in their own deaths!" I made this statement six years ago at a meeting of the American Psychological Association's sister organization, The United States Psychological Association.[4] Many gasped. But the truth of this theory has been borne out many times.

As different as they are from each other, these three professionals shared one significant characteristic: suspicious bravery. Routinely, they unflinchingly confronted innumerable sociopaths, psychopaths, and the otherwise criminally insane in their respective communities. To make matters worse, they squared off against, and helped incarcerate, several leaders of organized crime as well. Testifying in open court, they behaved in a manner that would certainly and inevitably trigger revenge impulses in the most disturbed elements of their community. There is no doubt that they were each the target of many murder attempts, one of which was certain to be successful. The only question was which felon would commit the act first.

It is important to realize that each of these three men were highly intelligent, culturally savvy individuals. It is highly improbable that they were unaware of the self-destructive consequences of their activities. Each had to understand the risks and the likely outcome of their crime-fighting activities. This being the case, it can be said that they colluded in their own inevitable demise.

In a sense, each found an elaborate way to kill himself while remaining true to his heroic self-idealization. They gave their lives for their clients. What an immeasurable gift! It thus behooves us to take account of this as we watch their valiant escapades in reruns. As you sit and enjoy the exploits of Jim Rockford, for instance, a profound sense of gratitude and tear-filled eyes are an appropriate emotional response.

[4] June 12, 1990, Room 232, Days Inn, Phoenix, Arizona.

Why **We** Watch

Below is another famous character with the results of their LPB (Life Probability Analysis), including their MLS (Mid-Life Snapshot). See chapter 3 for more details.

Goober Pyle Although he was certainly intellectually limited, perhaps even mildly retarded, Goober had sufficient social skills to function independently. His work as a mechanic was risky, however, due to the high probability that he would misdiagnose and blunder with some frequency. Add to this his constricted communication skills, shoddy personal hygiene, and discomfort with confrontation, and Goober is quite vulnerable to a work-related crisis. Along with his cousin Gomer, it was likely that before too long, he would become involved in a serious altercation involving an irate customer.

MLS: Goober eventually marries a depressed and irritable woman eleven years his junior, and they have two children. After several incidents involving his questionable mechanical skills, his auto repair business decreases to a bare minimum. The oil shortage in the 1970s, however, creates more profit in fuel sales. Goober becomes a franchise owner for a major national oil chain, installs the first self-serve pumps, and opens three more locations. He becomes wealthy. In 1984, he and Gomer are severely injured when a tanker truck explodes at their station. Now walking with a severe limp and as a result of extensive plastic surgery, he is unrecognizable to viewers.

Viewing Into Health

After you have established that you or a loved one has TBD, the question arises, "now what?"[5] What does Teletherapy suggest as a way to cure the person? For starters, we must point out the difference between being cured and being healed. Modern medicine seeks to cure illness and disease. Achieving a cure is not always possible for conventional medicine and, sadly, people continue to die. But with healing, a patient can attain inner peace and tranquillity regardless of the state of a cure. While it may not always be possible for medicine to cure someone, healing is available to all. Coming to terms with your illness means you accept what is possible and impossible.

But now, with Teletherapy, this distinction is on the verge of becoming obsolete. The promise of Teletherapy is that TBD can be cured and the patient completely healed all at the same time. According to Senior Teletherapy Medical Advisor Neil McNeil, "there is no doubt that all TBD symptoms disappear and an incredible sense of inner quiescence is almost always reached."[6] Teletherapy stands behind its treatment of TBD and challenges anyone to dispute its claims. "But they do so at their peril!"[7]

Final Caution

While Teletherapy is the premiere strategy for overcoming all television-based illnesses, it assumes no responsibility if your cure fails. Not everyone has the inner strength, the character, or the deft thinking necessary to apply these complex techniques. This is why attempting the Teletherapy Home Course is not always appropriate. Consult a Certified Teletherapist before beginning any viewing program. Through their extensive testing, they can advise you on how to proceed. If

[5] If the question that arose was "so what," reread the chapter on dysfunction. If this still has no effect on your personality, it is recommended that you send for the workbook that accompanies this volume and practice the suggested exercises.
[6] McNeil, an Itinerant Licensed Practical Nurse, has verified dozens of simultaneous cures and healings through Teletherapy.
[7] Threat made by author responding to a question by Channel 19 News, Lafayette, Indiana, January 1995.

they recommend institutionalization, do not refuse. Enter quietly and without resistance. If you hesitate, even for a moment, it can nullify all warranties and guarantees about your treatment.[8]

The bottom line is that the responsibility is the viewer's to watch television responsibly. If you develop a television-based illness, you have only yourself to blame. While this may seem to be a harsh assessment, it is nonetheless true. Ultimately, it would be a disservice to you if the issue was soft peddled. No, if the truth be told, with a few key exceptions, you, and not television itself, are responsible for how you have misused the medium.[9] Thus it is your responsibility to regain your psychological health.

[8] Ample court precedent includes "Ralph vs. Miller" '92, "Bickel vs. Miller" '94, "Pannell vs. Miller" '94, and several others.

[9] Two obvious instances of fault resting with television itself include the early TV shows *My Friend Flicka* and *My Mother the Car*. Each of these shows was laden with damaging psychological messages.

CHAPTER 8

Television and Fear of Death

Scoobie Doo and *The Flintstones'*
Doomsday Scenario

WARNING! PLEASE STOP READING NOW! DO NOT GO ANY FURTHER!

This chapter addresses deep and frightening issues: death and the fear of annihilation. In the words of Gomez Addams, "death, that's the biggie!"[1] Thus it is not for children or those who are in denial. If you are under the age of thirteen, or have difficulty accepting reality, you are advised to skip to the next chapter. But for those of you who consider yourselves deep, proceed with caution. Be aware that this section might raise difficult emotional issues. You might want to consult a therapist before you begin. On the other hand, if you are able to handle this subject, you are about to become an even deeper person than you already are.

Death Relaxation Exercise

In order to present this very challenging material, it is advisable to place yourself in a state known in Teletherapy as a Simulated Near Hypnosis. In fact, it would be unwise, and even dangerous to proceed unless you submit to this precautionary process. In this more relaxed condition, you have a better perspective on the entire matter of death.

1. Balance on one leg for a full minute, or until you feel an uncomfortable ache.
2. Switch legs, and repeat the procedure.
3. In this weakened position, bend forward and rest your hands on your knees.

[1] As retold by Herve Villechaize, April 5, 1979.

4. Breathing audibly and loudly, fill your lungs slowly, hold this breath, and exhale quickly. Repeat this three times.

5. Throughout the exercise, meditate on your death, letting the feelings of fear come to the surface first. Eventually, your inability to change the inevitable will give way to a sense of defeat and resignation. Although this induces some depression, it will ease the anxiety and allow greater functioning until the next panic episode.

You are now ready to proceed with the chapter.

We Are All Doomed

There is no question that we must all come to terms with death; no one escapes. Television has not shirked its responsibility in dealing with this greatest of all human challenges. From *The Addams Family* to *M*A*S*H*, TV has directly addressed the dilemma of demise. And you will be a richer person for having tackled this issue for yourself. The process begins with a conscious acceptance of the inevitability of death. Teletherapy joins the ranks of several other disciplines in acknowledging the fact that every human being will die. Further, it believes that this fundamental issue must be addressed from the television perspective.

Let's begin with an assessment of your understanding of death. Answer the following questions:

1. Have you ever experienced profuse sweating during *Quincy, M.E.?*
2. Do you find it hard to make eye contact with someone in the funeral home industry?
3. Do you count the "Chuckles the Clown" death episode of *The Mary Tyler Moore Show* among your top five favorite shows?
4. Does the smell of gladioli induce nausea?
5. Has any member of the cast of *Touched by an Angel* ever appeared in your dreams?
6. Are you frightened of throat lozenges?

If you answered yes to any of these questions, there is a good probability that you are repressing fears about the issue of death. It would be advisable to closely study the material in this chapter. As we proceed, the subject of death is divided into three more manageable issues: fear of death, the act of dying, and life after death.

Fear of Death

Are you afraid? Of *course* you are! Everyone is afraid. If, right now, you are not feeling deeply afraid, terrified really, then you have been overtaken by a well-known visitor, our old friend, Mr. Denial. And that's good! Although it is quite natural to be in dread fear at all times, it must be at an unconscious level. We could not function if we perpetually felt this terror consciously. In order to carry on with our lives, it is necessary to repress this foreboding about our death. Much of our energy is spent in this repressive effort. If, for example, you find that you often tremble during routine household tasks, or that your voice quavers while speaking with a retail clerk, your unconscious death dread is pushing its way into consciousness, causing these physical reactions. When this happens, repeat the Death Relaxation Exercise described at the beginning of the chapter.

One of the most effective strategies of repression is through self-distraction. You might have heard the phrase "amusing ourselves to death"? Perhaps a more accurate phrase would be "amusing ourselves from death." By distracting ourselves we are able to forget for the moment that we can be destroyed at any second. The possible death scenarios are endless, from a mundane car wreck, to an unpredictably elaborate scheme in which a strange European man picks us out at random and decides to sneak up and garrote us to death. This is the point of which a wide range of television shows, from *Cops* to *Murder She Wrote* confirms. There have been well over two hundred homicides within the circle of family and friends of Jessica Fletcher.[2]

We fear two basic categories of killers: Mother Nature and father revenge. The first fear is more primal, that untamed nature will annihilate you. One minute you are weed whacking, the next moment a sinkhole opens up and eradicates you from the physical plane. And all throughout, the nearby robin chirps without interruption in your backyard birch tree. Or there you are frolicking in the ocean and suddenly a shark devours you in front of the community. No thought, no

[2] Nick at Nite Labs has estimated that Jessica has spent well over fifty-six thousand dollars on floral arrangements to funeral homes.

remorse, no safety. Is it any surprise that we are in constant fear? No wonder we watch so much television so mindlessly. We are in need of anesthesia.

In response to this fear, Teletherapy suggests two distinct strategies. One is to use the healing power of escapist television, which emphasizes the more loving aspects of nature. This would include *Flipper, Gentle Ben,* and any rerun with tamed horses or domesticated wildlife, such as coyotes and ferrets. In addition, it is also helpful to watch the most gruesome nature shows on Discovery or public television, for instance. Try to watch programs showing wild animals chase, maul, and kill innocent elk and antelope. The reason is that it ultimately demonstrates humanity's ability to reduce the impact of these killer forces to a more controlled level of acceptance. These shows foster the reminder that we can and often do overcome some of the worst aspects of the murderous unpredictability of nature. In other words, we acknowledge that cheetahs can still kill us, but we usually don't encounter one in our neighborhood. While all of this is simply an illusion, it can facilitate coping on a daily basis.

Television Death Poem

The following verse was penned by Bill Curtis, a self-described "tele-poet" from southern Florida.

Excuse Me? I'm Dying Here!

excuse Me? I'm Dying Here!
morticia invites me, Fester repels me
excuse Me? I'm Dying Here!
herman incites me, Thing ignites me

excuse Me?
i don't remember asking you to surf the channels
i'm Dying Here!
do you have any care what I want to see?
EXCUSE . . .
ME? . . .
I'M DYING . . .
HERE!

Father Kills Best: Oedipal Television

Freud made clear that one of the most complex struggles in early human life is the one we play out within the "Oedipal Triangle." The actors in this psychodrama are the mother and father and child, and how the drama is played determines how well the child will mature. This theory says that the intense bond of love and intimate connection between the mother and child triggers a jealous rivalry with the father. While the mother is the god-being the child utterly trusts and adores, father, shunted off into the background in the birth experience, is the unknown stranger. The task for the child is to come to know the father. The child develops a deep-seated fear that the father, in a fit of jealous rage, will kill him as an interloper, a rival for the affections of mother. Eventually, the child must surrender his exclusive relationship with mother, and move away to seek his own intimate relationship. But the loss and denial last forever. This theme carries on through the life of the child who will later view all love relationships in terms of this denial of mother and the threatening jealousies of father.

What does all this mean? It explains just about everything, including all television shows. Seen through the lens of this Oedipal theory, we can instantly interpret the meaning of Bosley as a father figure on *Charlie's Angels*. We suddenly understand the profound tension between Archie and Meathead. We vividly see that Herbert T. Gillis's rage at his son Dobie was rooted in his wife's evident love for her son. It shines a light of understanding on everything from *Kung Fu* to *Perry Mason*. The theme underlying all these shows is the fear of father's wrath.

In response to Oedipal-based fear, Teletherapy suggests the following strategy. Immerse yourself in shows accentuating calm, nurturing parent figures. Spend time observing Ben Cartwright, Bob Hartley, John and Zeb Walton, and Dr. Cliff Huxtable. While this will probably have no real impact, it might provide momentary calm. The brutal truth is, there is nothing to be done about this fear. It is rooted so deeply in your unconscious life, that it will remain with you for the rest of your life. Only your actual death will bring relief—we think. You must learn to bear the weight of this inner fear that someone in a nurturing position will snap and kill you for reasons too complicated to comprehend. Watching television might not relieve the fear, but it will distract you with a powerfully effective anesthesia.

85

SCOOBIE DOO: "I See Too Much!"

For a great insight into the struggle with your death fear, watch a few episodes of *Scoobie Doo*. Notice that in every case, the teenage sleuths repeatedly charge into dangerous circumstances involving dangerous criminals, spies, even murderous ghosts and monsters. In each case, they face these risks without any apparent memory of their most recent, narrow escape.

But keep your eye on their dog, Scoobie. This animal is in perpetual terror for his life! His fear is far more exaggerated than any of the human beings around him. Why? One simple word: "repression!" Scoobie is unable to repress his fear of death. Like all animals, his prime instinct is survival. Any life-threatening situation would be immediately clear to him, and he would instantly flee. But here he is stuck with caretakers, upon whom he is dependent for his food, and they repeatedly expose him to the risk of death. What a dilemma for Scoobie!

In essence Scoobie is ever crying out, "We will die! I cannot pretend; I see too much!" Scoobie reminds us that although we are all at risk for death, humans have a great gift that allows us to repress this fear. We can ignore much of the frightening reality around us. Scoobie demands that we not take this great capacity for granted! And he has almost convinced Shaggy.

Create Your Own Teletherapy Death Poem

When you cannot express yourself because you are immobilized by fear of death, create your own poem to certain TV word references that could easily rhyme. Read this poem aloud to a trusted friend and ask for their comfort for your agony.[3]

For example, here is a simple, but quite moving poem submitted by Ms. Trish Coffey, an inpatient at the Teletherapy Clinic in Kearny, New Jersey:

Murder me? No, MURDER ONE!
Matlock overrules my accusers
But I grow weak and no one is here now
Where is Perry? Where is Wapner?
O NO! Even Little Joe—Jonathan is dead and gone!
Now who will show me the on-ramp to the Highway to Heaven?

Now you try it using these words and phrases: Twilight Zone, M*A*S*H, Mrs. Muir, Morticia.

The Act of Dying

The key to the fear of death is, of course, the act of dying. What is it? It is the demise of your physical body whereby your breathing stops, your heart ceases beating, and the light in your brain goes out. It is assumed to be an unpleasant experience, but we cannot be sure. It is certainly cause for grief and pain for those left behind. And herein lies a clue. The very phrase "left behind" assumes that the deceased has traveled to some other place or dimension. We cannot be certain of this either, but this is surely the hope we all harbor.

Television has approached the subject of death in two radically distinct fashions. On the one hand television is awash in death. Many shows depict dozens of

[3] Do not become demoralized after reading the professional poem on page 84. Mr. Curtis is a professional and you are not expected to create at the same level.

deaths, usually through violence. On the other hand, television often ignores death. Many shows shun the whole idea. Teletherapy believes that this mix is ultimately healthy for the viewer because we must strike a balance between facing reality and utilizing healthy denial so that we can function with hope and optimism.

See That Mushroom Cloud? Meet The Flintstones!

Ironically, one of the most futuristic television shows of all time was *The Flintstones*. Many viewers assume it depicts an ancient past. Nonsense! *The Flintstones* is actually a show about a terrifying future! The program first came on the air in 1960, at the very height of tension between the United States and the Soviet Union. Every citizen lived in dread fear of being annihilated in a nuclear war. School children participated in drills hiding under their desks while homeowners built bomb shelters in their backyard. It was a terrifying time.

What if the worst happened? Suppose there was a full exchange of missiles with Russia and indeed the earth was laid waste—the entire country was leveled by the blasts! Now imagine that a tiny remnant of people survived in small numbers across the land. As they picked themselves up and began the daunting task of rebuilding their lives, it is certain that they would re-create a middle-class life out of the primitive materials available from the now scorched earth. The civilization they would construct would look astonishingly like—Bedrock!

Thus *The Flintstones* is actually a fantastic dream vision of a post-apocalyptic American community that survived the nightmare of a nuclear holocaust! Next time you watch, you should feel profoundly grateful that *The Flintstones* did not become a reality for us! In fact, have you written anyone in authority to express your thanks? Why not send a note to the government and say "thank you for saying 'NO' to the Flintstones!"

Life After Death

One of the most significant contributions Teletherapy has made to humankind is its irrefutable proof of life after death. As of May 1993, no Teletherapist is in a position to refute this proof. The discovery was made at the Nick at Nite Satellite Laboratory in Las Vegas, Nevada, and confirmed dramatically at a catered lunch one afternoon at the Embassy Suites Hotel.[4] It also has involved thousands of hours analyzing show tapes, as well as testimony from hundreds of Teletherapy patients.

It is reassuring to know that television provided the avenue into the afterlife. This is fitting since television is most responsible for keeping thousands of characters alive and prospering as they remain timeless in their shows. Only the deterioration of tape and film could possibly threaten their existence. Even this has become nearly impossible with the advent of digitized processes and the transfer to computer technology. We believe that before too long, it will be possible to regularly communicate with dead television characters directly over the monitor of your combined television-computer screen. We are excited with anticipation for that inevitable day. Even if you die before it comes, we will all still communicate, but you will just do so from the other side. From a Teletherapeutic perspective, this will be no big deal.

---

[4] The direct contact through the television screen from beyond the grave in front of two dozen professional Teletherapists and hotel support staff by late actor Hugh Beaumont of *Leave It to Beaver* fame, May 14, 1993. He reported a fully embodied experience after death and assured us all that a television-type technology is a principle feature of the afterlife environment.

Teletherapy and the Afterlife

These are the six principle Teletherapeutic Proofs of life after death:

1. The persistent failure of Dick Clark to physically deteriorate.
2. Shockingly persuasive stories told on *Unsolved Mysteries*.
3. Personal testimony of Near-Death Experiences by major celebrities.
4. Certain complex interpretations derived from episodes of *Empty Nest*.
5. Evident conviction felt while watching *Highway to Heaven*.
6. Almost commonplace sightings of Telly Savalas by hundreds at the Universal Sheraton Hotel in Los Angeles.

Television and a Life Without Fear

The answer to the ongoing dilemma about human fear is to watch and study television. Simply put, it is impossible to be worried about your demise while in the middle of watching *Wheel of Fortune*. It is not likely that your palms will sweat in nervous anxiety while you are focusing on an episode of *Who's the Boss?* In general, any television viewing is preferable to sitting around in agonizing contemplation about the thousands of catastrophic events that could befall you at any moment. But some care should be taken. For example, if you find yourself needing distraction while in the middle of a fear spell, it would be unwise to sit through a show that features a depressed lead character such as *My Three Sons* or *Starsky and Hutch* or even *Jake and the Fatman*. Select programs where the lead character is in strong denial, repressing their fears. Among these are *Full House, I Dream of Jeannie,* and *Gomer Pyle*. If you are in doubt about a certain show, call the Teletherapy Content Hotline in Kansas City.

Face the truth: You are going to die, if not sooner, then a little later. Even if you are destined to live for many more years, it will go by in a flash. It will speed before you in a gale of depressing velocity. The sirocco winds of demise are blowing all the time. You cannot escape. So accept it and move on with the little time you have left. Watch television intelligently and try to calm yourself.

CHAPTER 9

Television and the Paranormal

The Quest for Mystery

Yearning for More

No matter what we have, we will always want things we do not have. This simple, painful truth about the human condition is one we all recognize, but fight hard to deny. Even when we are successful and accumulate massive amounts of material goods, it is shocking that we still yearn for more. In an interview with the *New York Post,* sweepstakes winner Lou Chiarella, a supervisor for the Brooklyn Union Gas Company, wrote the following: "Man, I can't believe it. I got everything, and it's still not enough. I yearn for more. I'm tellin' ya, I yearn!"[1]

Material possessions cannot garner happiness. This is a basic tenet of Teletherapy's philosophy about the human condition. Human joy can only be achieved by satisfying our higher, transcendent needs. Until we quench our thirst for spiritual satisfaction, we will always feel a sense of emotional impoverishment. And nobody wants to see that happen. Television is often misunderstood as celebrating our basic drives while allegedly ignoring our higher inclinations.

Television as a Divining Rod

Television is perhaps the most under-used resource in our search for higher meaning. In the words of C. P. Chesterton, "Television is perhaps the most under-used resource in our search for higher meaning."[2] Yes, right there in your den is

---

[1] Lou misread his letter from Ed McMahon. Based on seeing the words "you are already a winner," he started purchasing items with his credit cards to "get the ball rolling" until his winnings came. He was forced to return over $26,000 in goods and services.

[2] "Looking for Higher Meaning Without Television," C. P. Chesterton, Teletherapy Journal, January 1996.

the answer to that groaning from within. While external reality slams the door on supernatural phenomena, television waves you through to a world without limits. Television provides answers to all life's key questions. In the last decade alone, using the analytical tools of Teletherapy, Nick at Nite's scientists have proven conclusively that there is life after death; shown that there is alien life among us; and demonstrated that past life regression is a real thing.[3] These secrets were revealed through certain episodes of *The Outer Limits* and *Quantum Leap*.

Whether you are a fan of *Unsolved Mysteries, The X-Files,* or *Sightings,* you know that where hard science says no to your suspicions, television says yes! Television reflects your own beliefs that there is more to this world than we experience with the limited system of our senses. If you hold beliefs that are considered strange and eccentric by your family and peers, remember, Michael Landon was on your side. So is Dionne Warwick, Nancy Reagan, and singer Perry Como. Teletherapy rejects the puffed-up pronunciations of all pretenders to skepticism. Teletherapy reminds you that even the word skeptic appears right before the word "skerry" in the dictionary. And skerry is defined as "an isolated rock or reef in the sea." Don't be drawn away from the shore of sanity into the sea of insignificance called skepticism. Remember, skeptics are like skerries, in other words, jerks!

Mrs. Muir's Delusions

"It is a national tragedy that *The Ghost and Mrs. Muir* is not shown more often in reruns. We are a poorer people as a result. Millions of lives could be healed with this powerful program." This is a statement made by the author at a Congressional hearing on the impact of television.[4] Although this testimony was never placed into the record, its truth cannot be denied. This show was a potent teaching tool about the balance between paranormal reality and delusional disorder. It showed us that our fantasies can become so vivid that they actually take on their own reality. And this is not necessarily a bad thing.

---

[3] See "Teletherapeutic Analysis of the Psychic Friends Network," *Teletherapy Men's Quarterly,* May 1995. Also, see the report entitled "Study of Dream Analysis with the Cast of *Designing Women,* October 1992.

[4] Made on the steps of the Capitol to a gathering of other rebuffed witnesses, January 1994.

Captain Gregg, clearly a projection of Mrs. Muir's inner yearnings, offered her real advice and counsel to guide her life. She actually made many decisions based on the "higher wisdom" of this apparition. Although in reality these tips were coming from within her own unconscious, they were not readily available to her by her own will. She had to concoct the presence of a ghost in order to make her inner knowledge and wisdom accessible to her conscious life. This means that the apparition was real after all. While it originated from inside herself, the phantasm became real as an intermediating vehicle between her unconscious and conscious life, between her inner and outer self.

Only television can create such vivid realities. Thus, on television, ghosts do exist and communicate with mortal beings. Teletherapy fully accepts ghosts, UFOs, alien life forms, and all other spiritual, psychic, and paranormal phenomena as really existing and constituting total truth. To deny the existence of any of these phenomena is to admit your denial and dysfunction. Teletherapy goes beyond science and sees itself as a suprascience, which is universally superior to all other sciences combined. It takes a backseat to no other science, including chemistry, biology, physics, and metaphysics. None of these other, vaunted, so-called disciplines has anything useful to say about *The Ghost and Mrs. Muir*. In the words of Teletherapist Lenny Rockefeller, alleged grandson of the late Nelson,[5] "Teletherapy is quickly losing interest in any further dialogue with the other hard sciences. Frankly, they bore us."

Past-Life Regressions: From Squiggy to the Pharaoh

Past-life regression is a controversial therapy technique whereby the patient, under hypnosis, recalls vivid memories of a previous life. Frequently, they return to an ancient life experience in a foreign setting. Many of these experiences occur in ancient Egypt, for instance. In addition, the regressed patient will typically appear as an individual of royal status. Few appear as anonymous, humble citizens such as plumbers, food vendors, or bookkeepers. In a recent research study at the Nick at Nite Regression Clinic in Boca Raton, Florida, a startling finding was

[5] Paternity pending.

Why We Watch

STAR TREK's Vision: "Captain, I've Got to Have More Power!"

There was probably no better illustration of television's power to dream than *Star Trek*. For over a generation space exploration has been the relevant metaphor illustrating both our desires and fears about life itself. There are times when each of us feels that we are hurtling through inky black space, trying to find our way, exposed to unknown and often monumental odds. The excitement of *Star Trek* is that the opposition they encountered was always overwhelming, dwarfing human capacity. And yet, thanks to the combination of Jim's human spirit and Spock's analytical dispassion, they overcame all odds to survive and move on. This is how we feel in our lives as well.

If you are devoted to this program, it means that you see yourself on life's journey, which is taking you to places where no one has gone before. You view life's struggles as a series of great personal challenges, which demand all of your "Inner Kirk" and "Inner Spock" qualities. Failure means annihilation!

If you experience mild tension during this program, it means that you see yourself as a passenger on life's journey. You align yourself less with the leadership, such as Kirk, Spock, Scotty, and more with the anonymous entry-level worker whose responsibilities on the *Enterprise* include such mind numbing tasks as processing the recyclables or repairing chipped countertops.

If you are bored with this program, it means that you see yourself as a nonparticipant in life's journey. In essence, you have become simple baggage to be delivered to some unknown destination by the *Starship Enterprise*.

Thus, some people are living life on the Bridge, others are living life in the kitchen, and still others are living life in the cargo hold! Where are you?

that "Only 4 percent of all past-life regressions involved individuals from trades generally involving high perspiration. This was unexpected."[6]

In a growing trend that has past-life therapists scratching their heads, many patients are popping up in past lives within early television shows. Deep in their hypnotic state, they distinctly recall life as a neighbor of Lucy Ricardo, a wardrobe assistant to Ed Sullivan or, in one remarkable case, a nervous Native American, "Hekawi" adolescent with moderate acne living near "F Troop." This trend has triggered the involvement of Teletherapy. Within the last two years, more than 40 percent of all practicing Teletherapists have included past-life regression analysis in their regular clinical work. As a result, there has been an explosion of reported incidents of television-based memories.

Past-Life Regression: Leapfrogging Through TV

These are some of the most significant symptoms that you are stuck in a recent television past life, which prevents you from moving to an even earlier history:

1. Dreaming about Mesopotamia after watching *The Dukes of Hazzard*.
2. Intrusive thoughts about Anwar Sadat during a sitcom.
3. Persistent sense of déjà vu during commercials.
4. Inexplicable use of the preposition "thou" in routine conversations following *What's Happening!!*
5. You wear autumn colors when it is obvious to everyone that you are a winter.

Among the most amazing past lives brought forward in Teletherapy, none is more striking than that of Ms. Moretta Scott of Columbia City, Indiana. It seems that in her initial past-life regression, she spoke about her early life as Lorraine Squiggman, the unseen but very real mother of Andrew "Squiggy" Squiggman, neighbor of Laverne and Shirley. This woman, a tortured soul who was victimized by an emotionally withdrawn, military father and then a boisterous, emotionally explosive, salesman husband, suffered from depression. In conversations with her,

---

[6] "Past-Life Regression: Where Were They?" Section IV, p. 19, June 1993.

she revealed great guilt that her son Squiggy was probably brain-damaged as a result of inhaling the fumes of his father's excessive use of inexpensive cologne.

Suddenly, in an astonishing breakthrough, she moved further back in history and reported an even earlier life as the mother of an Egyptian king who was also unbalanced because of inhaling certain spice fumes! As the therapist noted, "It became obvious to me that this patient was only able to return to her earliest life with the help of television! In essence, she was 'leapfrogged' by a past life in a television show back into her more remote past. It made great sense, and yet, I was nonetheless thunderstruck!"[7]

Thus began a new chapter in the practice of Teletherapy, which can now rightfully claim credit as the premiere method of entry for all past-life regressions. Most Teletherapists are highly suspicious of any past-life analysis that has not been first triggered by a television-based "leapfrog." The reason is that television is such a universal influence on our culture that no one can see history except through the lens of television. In the words of the eminent Teletherapist-Philosopher Dr. J. P. Bachant, "You cannot get around television and into your past. It's impossible. You simply must go through it!"

Teletherapy with Victims of Alien Abductions

Frequently, testimony of victims of alien abduction include specific and dramatic references to television. Listen to the account of Ms. Linda Sweetman of Mahwah, New Jersey:

[7] Debriefing interview with Teletherapist Ian Schwartz, Gino's Delicatessen, Astoria, New York, September 1995.

I had just finished eating a three bean salad and laid down for a short nap. I was awakened by a blinding light, which felt warm and comforting. I felt myself being slowly lifted up from my bed. All of a sudden I was pulled toward the television in our bedroom and sucked into the screen. I passed through a world filled with television characters. But there was something different about them. At first I thought it was because they were suddenly three dimensional. But I later realized that it was something more. In each case, they were all healed from their afflictions. For example, I saw Uncle Joe from Petticoat Junction, but his voice was clear and smooth. I saw Tattoo from Fantasy Island, and he was over six feet tall. I saw Bosley from Charlie's Angels and the Angels were all in love with him. It was wonderful!

She went on to report that the aliens took her aboard their mother ship and had her explain the meanings of several popular shows. "I did the best I could, but after all, I am not a teletherapist. I do remember that they were especially interested in professional wrestling and Barney."[8]

It stands to reason that aliens bent on intrusion into the earthly realm would utilize the tools most readily available to them. It is simply not plausible to believe that the aliens would not make use of television. It is where most Americans can be found on most nights. They are also in a state of such focused concentration while watching that they are highly vulnerable to capture. Some of the clear signs of imminent abduction are blotted out by the distraction of television. Thus, the distinctive odors that precede abduction, as well as the eerie quiet and subtle pressure on the rib cage, which are the hallmarks of abduction, go unnoticed by the victim. Add to this the induced drowsiness associated with capture, and the normal state of television viewing becomes the ideal state for the kidnap.

In fact, there is a prominent theory in Teletherapy that many actual abductions go completely unnoticed because they are disguised as the viewing experience. One proponent of this radical theory boldly asserts that "every night, millions of viewers are taken aboard alien ships and returned to their den with no one the wiser. It is shocking that some of your favorite shows are not actually shows at all,

---

[8] Her husband Donald, who was in bed with her at the time, could not corroborate her story. Although he did say he had a restless nap, which he first attributed to a Focaccia sandwich. His wife swore that the aliens drugged him into submission. This cannot be confirmed.

but thinly veiled memories of your abduction!"[9] While not everyone is ready to concede these assumptions, Teletherapists are increasingly open to the idea that television is probably an unwitting participant in the growing epidemic of alien abductions.

Television-Based Symptoms of Alien Abduction

While there are many AMA-recognized symptoms of alien abduction, Teletherapy has added five specific television-related symptoms:

1. Vivid dreams, which include performance of cosmetic surgery on an anchor-man.
2. Active note taking during *Nova*.
3. Involuntary drooling during channel sign-off announcement.
4. Practicing minor, noninvasive surgery on pets after *ER* (for instance, removing cuticle buildup on your parrot).
5. Radical change from prior television viewing habits. (For instance, suddenly losing interest in watching NBA basketball to actively participate in religious clowning.)

Looking Deeper

In summary, we can quote the *Teletherapy Treatment Manual*'s statement about the other side of human experience. These so-called triple truths are the foundation of the science.

1. Television can be completely explained by Teletherapy.
2. All unexplained phenomena exist. If not, there would not be an urge to explain them.
3. Therefore, television can explain everything. The only limitation is the feeble-mindedness of the hearer.

[9] Dr. Glenn Sparks, Wheaton, Illinois, 1996.

Why We Watch

As a result of these accepted truths, we strongly urge every viewer to practice the religion of their choice and to seek broader understanding of their personal religious beliefs with the aid of Teletherapy. World without end. Amen.

The Hidden Meanings of Key Commercials

Here is a sample of the true meaning of selected famous commercial slogans. Expand this list and try your hand at interpreting them. Send the results to Nick at Nite.

• "We do it all for you!" A parody of the Golden Rule, which espouses unconditional love. Appealing to the insecurity of the codependent consumer, the surface message is designed to induce a guilt-driven purchase, but is really beckoning us to love each other through food.

• "Pizza, Pizza!" The cry of the Little Caesar is an outgrowth of his obsession with pizza pie. This is not just a deranged little man in a toga. This is Caesar, an obvious reference to our ego. The surface message is that when you have a craving, you must satisfy it or you are endangering the health of your inner self. Your sanity depends on it! At a deeper level, it is showing us that the path to personal peace is found in the study of ancient history.

• "It keeps going, and going . . ." This boast about the Energizer bunny, an obvious fertility symbol, seems to promise limitless potency for those who choose this battery. Speaking to people's sense of inadequacy, this product touches a very special spot for us all. Its true message of the marching rabbit is that you must seek joy or life's parade will pass you by!

• "Tastes great! Less filling!" Succinctly articulates the inner struggle between our higher and lower selves. On the one hand we all must respond to the drives of appetites for satisfaction and pleasure ("Tastes great," therefore more satisfying). At war with this is our drive for survival, to evolve and prosper by attending to long-term physical endurance ("Less filling," therefore more healthful). This product promises to attend to both drives. But in reality this commercial is mocking the notion that you can satisfy all your higher aspirations without having to include fine wine in your life.

CHAPTER 10

Television and Recovery

New Life
Through Teletherapy!

Recovery

It is most likely that reading this book has convinced you that you are very ill as a result of a lifetime of poor television viewing. Most of you have become aware that you have at least one serious, television-related illness, which needs treatment. If you are not convinced of this it most likely means that you have either skipped ahead to this section first, or you have only skimmed the material in the same shoddy manner you probably watch television. This is a shame because you are still in denial, and your family is ashamed of you. We call upon you to come to your senses and admit you are ill from television. Once you do this, you can begin your recovery back into full emotional health.

Do You Need to Recover from Television?

For those who remain unsure whether you are sick from poor television viewing, or for those who have skipped ahead in the text to this section, take this quick quiz to determine if you need Teletherapeutic Recovery. Answering yes to even one item means you need Teletherapeutic Recovery:

1. Do you read self-help literature out of sequence (e.g., skipping ahead to a later chapter)?
2. Do you try to avoid normal television through excessive viewing of PBS?
3. Have you ever experienced interrupted or nonsequential eye blinking while viewing?

4. Is selecting the right clothing an important part of your viewing preparation?
5. Do you experience a fuller understanding of television news while drunk?

The key to overcoming the sickness caused by years, even decades of poor viewing is to engage in a rigorous, ongoing program of recovery through the use of television itself. Usually this involves twelve steps, but can include more or less. Do as many as you can to start. As your enthusiasm grows, feel free to add your own steps. They can be highly personal, such as this one by a patient from Philadelphia: "Step 26: I committed myself to telling Eddie to 'shut up!' whenever he embarrasses me with his public belching."[1] These personal steps will help shape a custom-tailored program for your viewer illness. But be careful not to go too far. Adding too many can be harmful due to your deep-seated tendency to eventually relate to others inappropriately. There was a case in Louisiana where a codependent, after initial success, added sixty-one new steps. This completely reversed her recovery. For example, her fiftieth step was "made a conscious decision to make dinner at least twice a week for another codependent." Within a year she was hospitalized for exhaustion.[2]

The recovery process begins when you smash through your denial and admit that you are a sickened viewer. If you are unsure whether you are in denial, refer to the symptoms listed above and have several friends verify your unhealthy status. (Be careful that the friends offering the assessment are not abusive types as this could trigger a false negative reading.) Since you will be using your television as the tool of recovery, it is imperative that you prepare for the process by checking your cable or satellite connections, studying TV listings material, and making sure your reception has adequate clarity. Don't take this precaution lightly. There was a Teletherapy patient whose reception was quite hazy. As a result, he gleaned the wrong messages from his carefully prescribed viewing schedule and completely misinterpreted four *Matlock* episodes, thereby deepening his television-based depression![3]

[1] Name withheld by fee. (Although we can say that this was a fortyish brunette woman with a distinctive flower tattoo on her wrist.)
[2] Patty Ingleman, 4 Brady Lane, Linton, Indiana 46545.
[3] Sean Kelly Jones, 993 West End Ave., New York, New York 10025.

Even before you begin, do not take for granted that your diagnosis is accurate. Make sure you know what specific viewing illness you are dealing with before applying one of the recovery techniques. If, for example, you utilize the treatment techniques of Teletherapy for codependence for what is actually a television-based psychosis or some other television-induced personality disorder, it can result in fanning the flames of your symptoms unto death. This occurred on three separate occasions last year alone.[4] Be careful.

Once you have determined beyond doubt that you are an ailing viewer, you must then get into your recovery full throttle. Follow the prescriptions outlined in this chapter. If within thirty days, friends and family do not offer *unsolicited* comments about how much less chafing you are, then you must step up the process with the assistance of your own Teletherapist. Be careful not to seek these compliments yourself. The comments must come as a surprise. Often they are masked as generic compliments such as, "Did you lose weight?" or "Are you coloring your hair?" This is a clear early sign that your recovery is well underway.

Twelve Steps to Tele-Healing

If what you have read so far in this section has caused you to feel worse, remember, in your infected condition, anything can make you feel worse. This is because you are ill. Cheer up, "there is a path out of the forest of infection."[5] And that path is found right in front of you on the TV screen. As with other common psychological problems, Teletherapy asserts that you can "watch your way to wellness."[6]

With this assurance, here are the Twelve Steps to Tele-Healing from your addictive behavior.

---

[4] All three cases were residents of a nursing home in Ogden, Utah, who were participating in an unauthorized Teletherapy support group. In a misguided attempt to use Teletherapy, they watched *Studs* for fourteen hours straight. Teletherapy was cleared of any responsibility or wrongdoing.

[5] Jude Metcalf, from his poem, "o, your channel is killing my soul, o." Often called the "Poet Laureate of Teletherapy," Metcalf's book of verse, *Tee Vee* is available at Kinko's.

[6] Ron Gill, Senior Teletherapist, letter to Sumner Redstone, July 1995.

The Twelve Steps of Tele-Healing

1. We admitted out loud we were powerless over television, that our viewing had become unmanageable.
2. We came to believe that a channel more powerful than ours could restore our viewing to sanity.
3. We made a decision to turn our remote and our viewing over to the care of our Higher Channel.[7]
4. We made a searching and fearless moral inventory of our viewing.
5. We admitted to our Higher Channel, to ourselves, and to another viewer the exact nature of our inappropriate viewing.
6. We were entirely ready to have our Higher Channel remove all defects of viewing.
7. We repeat Step One, but louder.
8. We made a list of all shows we believe hurt us, and became willing to personally disengage from those who propose these shows to us.
9. We sought relief for our problems through a careful balance between Zen and selected patterns of weeping as prescribed by Teletherapy.
10. We repeat Step Three while at our workplace.
11. We sought through deep thinking and focused staring to improve our conscious contact with our Higher Channel as we understood it, praying only for emotional detachment and alleviation of sinful viewing.
12. Having had a spiritual awakening as the result of these steps, we tried to carry this message to other viewers on the World Wide Web and to practice these principles in all our affairs.

[7] Nick at Nite is considered the definitive option. Selecting another network would be considered a self-destructive and inappropriate choice. Nick at Nite is a nontoxic, racially inclusive, multi-creedal, and gender-neutral channel.

Rerun Therapy: Re-Viewing Your Past

One of the cutting-edge developments in all therapies is the "reconstructive narrative." In this exercise, the patients look back in their memory at their life's story. They then analyze that story and reinterpret it for themselves. For example, after many years of believing that their mother was completely inadequate, they try to achieve a more balanced view of her by bringing some of her positive qualities out into the open. Without denying her real failings, the patient seeks a more balanced opinion, which includes positive qualities they have unfairly ignored.

Teletherapy actively uses this same technique to correct many of the distortions of our viewing. We call it rerun therapy or more casually, rerunalysis. It has already changed  the lives of millions of people. It starts with the premise that, as a child, you were ill equipped to properly view television. The messages you took from your favorite childhood shows are almost always inadequate, distorted, and harmful to your development. These distorted memories stick with you. Full maturation can only be achieved when you revisit these shows and see, through adult eyes, the more complete messages of the shows. When you reconstruct your view to include the good and bad in a better balance, you will change as a person.

For example, read this excerpt from the personal journal of Laurie Robertson:

> When I was seven years old, I watched a full season of *I Dream of Jeannie*. I learned that, if you are very lucky, someone with magical powers can come into your life to help you. Years later, when as an adult I watched the show

again in reruns, I learned that men naturally desire a relationship with a beautiful woman who will serve their needs and cater to their every whim. I was tortured by the inconsistency of these two conflicting messages. But thanks to Teletherapy's rerunalysis, I was able to bridge the two, and a whole new interpretation emerged. The show is actually telling us that the great power of women ultimately cannot be contained. Jeannie would eventually smash her bottle and all hell would break loose!

Although this is a complete misreading of the show, the point is that this patient was able to rewrite her personal history through Teletherapy. Jeannie's bottle is central to her identity and to smash this means her death. Thus Robertson's interpretation actually meant that she felt Jeannie was suicidal, and this is not the case at all. Eventually she understood the show's meaning, an adolescent male fantasy about the ideal relationship: "I want a beautiful woman in my life but, when I'm tired of her, I want her to return to her bottle." The show is about the impulse to contain your loved one and thereby preserve and stunt her.

In early tests of the rerunalysis treatment technique at the Nick at Nite Labs, the impact on the patients has been remarkable. The only side effects discerned are minor, including increased foot odor and discoloration around the eyes. But as Nick at Nite's Senior Cosmetologist Dr. Tamara Downham noted, "Darkened eyes is a small price to pay for full recovery, and besides, with shoe pads and proper makeup, no one has to know you are in rerunalysis."[8]

Do You Need Rerun Therapy?

If you are unsure whether you could benefit from rerun therapy, note these classic symptoms:

1. Unable to name one character flaw in Aunt Bea (or, in contrast, strong feeling that Aunt Bea is a fraud and a phony).
2. Believe that Richie Cunningham never rebelled.
3. The thought of Mary Richards's face contorted in rage physically sickens you.

[8] Interview at the Nick at Nite Cosmetology Clinic, Secaucus, New Jersey, May 1995.

4. Excessive, boisterous laughter during *Eight Is Enough*.
5. Strong feelings of affection toward Al and Peg Bundy.
6. Keen interest in scenes involving Detective Lacey and her husband Harvey.
7. Persistent fantasies of violence during *thirtysomething*.
8. Riveted attention to detail while watching *Too Close for Comfort*.
9. Intrusive thoughts about your father while watching *Monday Night Football*.
10. Strong desire for serious discussion about the plot in *Three's Company*.

Relapse!

In any program of healing, we are dealing with the weak and shameful human will. This means that there will inevitably be failure, or in technical terms, relapse! If you have been involved in healing through Teletherapy, then you have already experienced the amazing high of good viewing health. Thus, when you relapse, you are crashing from an unprecedented and dizzying emotional height. The sheer distance of the fall can be nearly deadly. One minute you are watching television as a healthy, informed viewer, the next you are aimlessly channel surfing, looking for the cheapest stimulation possible. Before long, your personal habits deteriorate, your skin becomes sallow, and your hair thin and mousy. It is obvious to everyone that you are, in the words of that classic song by the Archies, ". . . back on the road to Telehell."[9]

There is only one way to respond to a relapse. You must recommit your life to the healing strategies available only through certain herbs and medications or the more certain treatment of a qualified Teletherapist.[10] Such treatment involves returning to the root of your problem—early childhood television viewing. It begins, of course, with a complete inventory of your past and present viewing. The Teletherapist will then recommend a re-immersion back into the television of those formative years as described above. But the twist will be that while you will

---

[9] Unreleased single "Telehell" from an unreleased album entitled *Telehell*, 1971.

[10] As this book went to press, there was an ugly incident in Texas where a phony group opened a Teletherapy clinic in the Dallas area. The individuals involved were not qualified Teletherapists and were in actuality perpetrating an elaborate insurance scam. They were arrested on a 91-count indictment.

watch many of those same programs, the Teletherapist will have you add into the mix certain other programs, which you clearly missed. The result is a corrective emotional experience for you. When you reconstruct your reality as experienced through proper television viewing, you become completely cured.

If, for example, when you were a young child and were an avid fan of *The Beverly Hillbillies* on CBS, it is obvious that you therefore missed most of *The Mod Squad,* which ran at the same time on ABC. The result is that you were never allowed to experience those crucial *The Mod Squad* lessons. In Teletherapy, this is known as a "view clash," and it represents a crucial developmental gap in your maturation. It is highly probable that most of your current aberrant behavior and dysfunction is rooted in view-clash problems. So each Friday while you might

have been riveted to *Bosom Buddies,* you were quietly starving for the critical life lessons to be gleaned from *The Dukes of Hazzard.* The loss is more than simply one less viewer for CBS. The real loss is for the psyche of you and everyone who missed the teaching of this great show.

Remember, through Teletherapy, you can revisit that childhood. There is no reason to be hypnotized; you can simply opt for a carefully planned program of re-viewing and become the mature person you have always aspired to be but failed to become.[11] But it is important to seek the help of a professional. Suppose, for instance, you set about watching some shows you missed in childhood without guidance. You might fool yourself into thinking that this will make up for any

---

[11] Hypnosis during Teletherapy can accelerate your healing but, for some, serious side effects can include permanent loss of short-term memory.

Five Tips for Healthy Viewing

As part of your recovery process, try to incorporate these five strategies into your regular viewing:

1. At least once a week, watch *The Jerry Springer Show* with the sound off and religious music playing in the background.
2. When watching reality-based programs such as CNN or *Nightline,* give an affirmation hug to another person at each commercial break.
3. Using a standard meter, write at least one poem each week about a favorite television character and send it to them (if they are deceased, ask that it be forwarded to a living relative).
4. Start a discussion group analyzing parallels between television characters and real people in your community. Offer an opportunity for your findings to be publicly reported.
5. Spending at least six hours per week, make a one-month, close study of a rerun from your childhood, analyzing its impact on your personality. Write a five-page, single-spaced paper outlining your findings and have friends and family evaluate and grade your work.

deficits in your personality. You would be wrong and walking on dangerous ground. Teletherapy is not easy, and its treatment benefits are only guaranteed under the watch care of a qualified professional. So while you are watching *The Dukes of Hazzard,* living in a fool's paradise, it could well be that what you actually need is a massive dose of *Hogan's Heroes* instead. What a disaster you have inflicted upon yourself as a result of trying to cut corners and save a few dollars. It could literally shorten your life. You can do a great deal of harm to your own psyche and the mental health of your family by careless re-viewing in a lame attempt to correct your view-clash problems. It simply will not work.

Dream Analysis Case File

Here is the second illustration of a dream and Teletherapy's analysis of it.

I dreamed that I was backstage at *The Ed Sullivan Show* waiting to perform. There was great pressure for me to do well, and I was petrified. But the worst part was that I had no idea what I was supposed to do. I had no talent! Should I dance? Sing? Tell a joke? What? I heard booing from the audience and Ricky Ricardo came off stage sweating. He looked at me and said, "That's a rough crowd out there! Good luck." I was introduced and went onstage. I stared at the silent audience and I broke down crying. I turned to Ed and said, "I'm sorry, I have no talent!" He broke into a big smile and said, "We know!" Then he and the entire audience burst out laughing. I looked down at the crowd and noticed my parents were in the front row laughing along with everyone else. I woke up.

—Ms. Barbara Axelrod,
Fairfield, Connecticut

Teletherapy's Interpretation: This dream touches on a common theme—the fear of being exposed as a fraud. In almost every case, this kind of dream also includes the fact that you are naked in front of the crowd. The fact that you do not mention this either means you are lying or in denial. In either case, you are living in dread fear that you have no real ability and that sooner or later your ineptitude will be shown to the world. Ed Sullivan represents the ultimate illustration of showcasing talent. Since you are humiliated in this most public forum, it means that you are suffering from grandiosity in your need to have the world see your incompetence. The presence of your parents is significant. They know your inadequacies better than anyone. Thus, their participation adds validity to the dream. Perhaps you really do not have any talent after all. We recommend long-term therapy and career counseling.

Good Luck!

Just prior to going to press with this text, the scientists at the Nick at Nite Labs carefully reviewed the material to check for spelling errors and misstatements of fact. To our delight, we discovered none. This means that the material in this book has delivered on its initial promise to completely cure you through television and assure you that you will be rich within thirty-six months. We have done our part. If you are not experiencing the great healing powers available through Teletherapy, it is evident that you are doing it wrong. Reread the book and reapply the techniques found here. You can be sure that if applied correctly, the program will work, guaranteed.

For those whose lives have been altered through the use of this book, we urge you to write to us at Nick at Nite and tell us your story. While we cannot pay you, we do reserve the right to use it in our teaching material and to freely share your name and address. In addition, we might contact members of your family or coworkers in order to verify the veracity of your account. Failure to prove your cure through Teletherapy might result in disconnection of your cable service or even criminal prosecution. Be careful to only include the truthful account of your cure.

We also urge you to contact your local media and encourage them to write stories about Teletherapy as a way to spread the news about this amazing new healing system. If possible, try to persuade a local technical college to begin a training program for Teletherapy in your community. The world is crying for the answers that only television can provide. Nick at Nite can provide all the assistance necessary to ensure that a fully licensed, certified program is put in place. If you do not take these steps within the next two months, there are serious doubts about the efficacy of your cure. You might be in the midst of a relapse. So get busy. And for all of you who have read the entire book and practiced the program fully, congratulations on becoming a healthy viewer and purging the toxic messages built up through years of sick viewing. Your family will not recognize your personality within a couple of months. But you can help explain what has happened to you while sailing across the lake in your yacht!

PART 2

Teletherapy's Profiles

of the 30 Most Psychologically Misunderstood Television Programs in History

At a recent conference on television psychology, I delivered a paper entitled: "We Are All Three Stooges." It received a strong response. One prestigious journal called it "mind boggling!" So I have decided to offer it to you here. It will serve as a foundation for the individual program analyses, which follow in this section. It demonstrates the analytical power of Teletherapy when applied to any media. I deeply believe in the truth of what I am about to share. If you care about humanity, you will believe, too.

The Three Stooges represent three dimensions of a human personality. Yes, we all have three stooges within ourselves. First, there is the "Moe Within." He is the assertive dimension, which is compelled to lash out aggressively at the stupidity and incompetence we experience around us. Like an angry infant, Moe cannot tolerate being denied his needs. His reaction to frustration is to immediately attack with slaps, pokes, and pulls. Moe is determined to punish and smash down the fool who confronts him. Each of us has this angry, "Moe-part" inside ourselves.

Then there is the "Larry Within." Larry is the often-slapped man, the victim of Moe's enraged lashing out. Even Larry's hair invites this abuse, seeming to shout, "here, pull me, rip at my head, poke me!" This is the unconscious voice that blames the self for all the difficulties we encounter. This "Larry-part" continues to confront the Moe for the purpose of meting out the punishment he feels he deserves. And, of course, Moe instinctively obliges with the invited abuse.

And we all have a "Curly Within." Curly is the chaotic, out of control man. He represents the psychotic dimension of the self that cannot manage life. Curly is the man who hops around, spins in circles, and cries "woo, woo,

113

woo." This is clearly the behavior of a psychotic person. Each of us fears this "Curly-part" of the self. One minute we are in our office handling the pressures of work and life, and the next minute we are shouting "nyuk, nyuk, nyuk" to our coworkers and drumming a tune with our fingers on our throats. This is the terrifying dimension of the self that we work so hard to keep buried.

What about you?

Think about your own personality. Is your dominant character trait aggression? Then you have a strong Moe dimension. For you, it is important to encourage your Larry to rise. Or perhaps you are a depressed type with poor self-esteem. Then you need to give greater voice to the Moe within yourself. If you identify with Curly, it is my hope that you seek professional help as soon as possible for the purpose of finding the Moe-Larry balance you so desperately need.

Assess your situation. Are you primarily a Moe, a Larry, or God forbid, a Curly? Work on the balance. Remember, separately they are stooges, but collectively, they are a fused, healthy individual. And so with you. If you are not living a healthy balance, you too are simply a stooge. Good luck in all your future endeavors.

Teletherapists are constantly asked the question, "Which are the most psychologically misunderstood television programs in history?" In response to this important query, we have assembled a list of twenty-five shows, which we feel are television's most psychologically misconstrued programs. These Teletherapeutic analyses were collected from our case files kept in our main library in Cozumel, New Mexico. The list is not an opinion of the best quality programs. It is simply a collection of some television fare that is repeatedly misinterpreted.

If you are not in Teletherapy and prefer to watch television in a mindless fashion, these programs contain subtle unconscious messages that are guaranteed to elevate your ego energy without your even being aware that it is happening. In watching these shows, we recommend that you choose one of two distinct approaches. If you are currently in Teletherapeutic treatment, make a close study of the information in this section. Keep a journal of your own impressions about this material. Share your feelings, thoughts, and fantasies with your Teletherapist. Create meaningful symbolic rituals based on what these analyses are teaching you.

However, if you have no intention of engaging in Teletherapy (and what a shame you have chosen complacency and to wallow in your own sick woundedness!), we recommend that you read the analyses of these television shows, and then immediately try to forget all this information as soon as possible. Resume viewing them in your previous, mindless fashion. You can get well in spite of yourself. Although we prefer to only be associated with members of the first group, either approach will work.

The A-Team
(1983-87)

An elaborate, adolescent rebellion fantasy, this show depicts the inner desire of the children to throw off the oppressive yoke of parental authority. The dictatorial, persecuting authorities in the Army, who are out to find and jail the A-Team, represent the despotic parents. In a strong family, the parents, like the military authorities, are typically viewed as possessing nearly limitless power, with a long reach into our lives. To stand up and challenge our parents, like challenging the authority of the United States Army, appears to be an overwhelming task. Our feeble attempts at rebellion usually end in failure. Even in circumstances where the parents are sniveling and weak-willed, it will not take long for the civil authorities, serving as backup cavalry to the irresolute parents, to step in and crush the child's defiance. Thus, the child engages in active fantasies whereby they somehow prevail over their parents. The *A-Team* embodies this fantastic wish. In this show, the characters have been unfairly accused of misdeeds. Instead of taking the consequences passively, they rise up and act out their rebellion. This is the same strong wish of every child who has been grounded.

What is different about the *A-Team* is that it involves us in a community of other oppressed individuals, specifically, our siblings. The intense bond between brothers and sisters is often underestimated. In a family that is ruled by stern, autocratic, and perhaps unjust parents, it does not take long before the conditions emerge that foment revolution. As you watch the show, you imagine that, along with your brothers and sisters, you are a member of this highly skilled team of warriors seeking justice and cowering the despots.

It is helpful to identify which of the characters most captivates you. Are you

Hannibal, the leader? Perhaps you are B.A. (Mr. T), the strong and enraged one. Or are you "Howling Mad" Murdock, deranged from your suffering under the burden of unjust authority? You can learn a great deal about yourself, your family, and your current difficulties with authority by studying *The A-Team*.

The Addams Family
(1964–66)

Each one of us knows intellectually that we can die at any moment. Any second now, you, or someone you love, might be annihilated by the random eventualities of a brutal environment. Whether hit by a truck, or by breathing in a killing contaminant, we are destined for demise. Even at best, we simply rot away. Well, how do you cope with this unsettling reality? By repression, that's how. Simply put, we cannot consciously think about this terrifying reality and still continue to function as productive people. Just what would happen if our family broke through the repressive barrier that protects us from living in constant terror of our inevitable death? Suppose they couldn't shake off the awareness. What would they become? *The Addams Family* is one answer.

Running during the same years as *The Munsters, The Addams Family* was far more bizarre from a psychological standpoint. The Munsters were a family of physically challenged individuals who were attempting to fit into the mainstream culture. But the Addamses did not fit in at all. They were detached socially and culturally. The program postulates an alternative strategy for coping with mortality. Suppose we simply invite death to come? Suppose we revel in its presence? Suppose it is not the final answer it purports to be? Suppose we live out the Halloween ritual as a mundane assumption? Suppose there is another reality that in fact uses death to embark on a transitioning moment into a greater reality? What if death ushers us in to its own full culture, one superior to our own? If such is true, and they seem to believe this, then the Addamses are quite right to be laughing at us.

But what is the cost to them? The Addamses have sacrificed their place in the human community. They have chosen to gamble that human grouping is less essential for full health than we now assume. They are saying to the rest of us:

"Although participating in the human family is helpful, it pales in comparison to fully bonding with the community of the dead." The Addamses are inviting us to join them in a new world they have discovered to be rich in physical and spiritual treasures.

My fear for this family is the fate of the children. What about Pugsley and Wednesday? It is one thing for Morticia, Gomez, and Fester to make this choice, but there are significant consequences for the children. The impact of their home life could do irreversible damage to their chances of becoming part of American society if they so desired. The preoccupation with death and its sexual seductions has disconnected them all from others. By their own hand they have become an "abnormal" family by almost every acceptable measure. The children will suffer the consequences far more than their parents, including cultural withdrawal, social isolation, and a cruel ostracism. They are likely to wilt under the pressures at school and will most likely endure severe occupational stress as adults. Because of their extreme disconnection from others, these children would almost certainly be at high risk for adult character pathology and its attendant deviant behavior. Very sad for everyone.

The Adventures of Ozzie & Harriet
(1952–66)

The Nelson family foreshadowed the direction television would take in the next millennium. In a premonition of the 1990s and beyond, this show boldly obscured the line between fact and fiction. In an uncanny way, it used this blurring to play out its most provocative psychological theme: the loss of the American father. Who is Ozzie?

This was the first family of American television. But it is hard to discern what is real and what is story. Were they a real family masquerading as others, or were they a fictional family borrowing from true lives? The show was a curious blending of fact and fiction about the Nelson family. They used their real names, involved their real children, and portrayed their real relationships for the viewer. Yet there was nothing real about their life circumstances on the show. While they portrayed an "average" white, middle-class suburban family of the 1950s, in truth the Nelsons were an active show business family, wholeheartedly dedicated to succeeding as television stars. Students looking for early evidence that television alters truth can find it here.

Of far greater import, however, is the issue of the American father. Ozzie Nelson is a prototype for the lost American male. A victim of the industrial revolution, the male was separated from his family. He has been gone so long that, even when he returns and is perpetually around, no one seems to notice him. Ozzie has no vital role, no meaning. A bell tolling the loss of the Western European father. Where is he? The American father has no family function, no home job, no internal career. In the family he has lost all meaning and purpose. Like Ozzie, he is superfluous to the family except that as a figurehead he is present.

This painful truth is acted out here because Ozzie enacts this role. Father Ozzie produced the show, orchestrated its success, managed the family's rise to stardom. Yet he refuses to write in a fictional role for himself. Instead he is the father who is always home, ever available at all hours of the day, eerily idle. In his true life, Ozzie went to law school, but never practiced law. He refused to play out the prepared role in real life. Ozzie says to American fathers, "You are lost to the family. It doesn't matter that in your reality you go off each day and work at your job. As far as the rest of the family members are concerned, you might as well be out in the backyard like me."

Ozzie's ubiquitous presence also serves the purpose of enacting a deep wish by the spouse and children, a wish for the father to be there rather than be absent. Is this a manifestation of Ozzie's guilt combined with a need to be taken care of by the rest of the family? Obviously he is providing for them economically. Or is he? Perhaps he inherited wealth and so feels like a fraud. Is he really capable of taking care of them all? All these questions point to the painful predicament of the American father.

The Adventures of Superman
(1951–57)

Not only is Superman a woman's ideal male figure, but he is the perfect male fantasy as well. Superman is every man's narcissistic ideal image. "I am perfect and, tragically, just like Superman I am trapped behind this emasculated visage of a mild-mannered nonentity. Oh woman, if only you could see the real me! I too am a Superman!"

Superman expresses man's deepest fantasy, to be the invincible warrior, dedicated to good deeds. As adolescents, we thrill to the dream that we, too, will emerge a perfect male specimen. What works especially for our unconscious is Superman's disguise. We relate less to a naked display of power and more to a Clark Kent facade masking the Superman inside. Most men feel more like Clark: mild-mannered, timid, easily underestimated. So this becomes a splendid depiction of the aggressive drive of men. In essence most men are saying, "Don't be fooled here. Behind this mild-mannered exterior I am full of enormous power." Thus, while women are drawn to Superman as an object of desire, the rescuing father, men vicariously identify with him in narcissistic fantasy.

Superman had more than simply enormous physical strength. He had other enviable powers as well. For example, he had penetrating vision and hearing. He could see through someone and hear almost everything. Nothing was hidden from him. Physical prowess, penetrating insight, ability to listen, emotional sensitivity: These are qualities that make a man irresistible to women. Oh how men fantasize themselves to be this ideal man. It is all so charged with libidinal power!

But there was a problem. Such a seductive portrayal, a real Superman, was too intense for public airing in the staid era of the 1950s. A television Superman needed to be muted. This is clearly seen in how Superman and Lois are portrayed. In the earlier animated *Superman,* both characters were more powerful. With lantern eyes and an seductive smile, Lois was beautiful and sexy, a credible suitor for the greatest male on earth. It is no surprise that Clark is infatuated with her, longing to reveal his true identity. But for television Lois conforms to the times and is cooled off. She became more doughty and drab, with little sexual allure. The romantic chemistry was all but removed. Television adapted to the demands of society. So again, Superman did what was asked of him, for you and me, for America! Thanks Superman!

Why We Watch

Batman
(1966–68)

Batman is best understood psychologically when contrasted with the other principle, fictional male ideal, Superman. By having both available to us, we glean an
intriguing picture of our neurotic self and our idealized, non-neurotic self.
Batman, appropriately cloaked in darkness, offers a glimpse at our neurotic ideal.
This is the best we could become without therapy.

Batman is a more human superhero than Superman. To begin with, he has no
superhuman powers. This certainly raises the stakes when he exposes himself to
the lethal dangers of his crime-fighting avocation. He is overcoming self-doubt by
the force of great courage. Consequently, Batman is a more accessible hero for us.
This does not make him preferable, per se, just distinct. Batman serves a different
purpose for us than does Superman.

A key ingredient here is the interplay between fantasy and reality. Batman is a mirror image of Superman in this regard. He always appears in disguise in his superhero life. For him to emerge as a hero, his real identity has to remain hidden. This is the opposite of Superman, who is disguised in his non-hero life, his non-reality. Bruce Wayne is really Batman; Clark Kent is not the real Superman.

For us, there are times when identification with Superman's invincibility is helpful as it connects with our narcissistic grandiosity. For most of us, Batman more accurately reflects where we are in the struggle against personal fear and repressed anger. Like him, our real self is a shy, civil Bruce Wayne, aspiring to material success, but tempered by strict boundaries against expressing anger. In fantasy, we imagine ourselves to be avenging heroes who crush villains and save the weak. But we don't for a second believe this to be our true identity. Most of us feel we are more like Clark Kent in reality than we are Superman. Therefore, Bruce Wayne more accurately reflects our self-assessment.

The two pose a juxtaposition of the human neurotic dilemma: It is the false me who is out there doing good and being powerful. Batman is neurotic, Superman is cured of neurosis. Bruce Wayne is Superman; Batman is Clark Kent. So the show beckons us out of ourselves. It says to us as it also calls to Bruce that our true self is indeed powerful. Batman can be our full-time identity. We too can be Superman. Bruce Wayne can become superfluous to our identity. If we will only lose our fear.

The Beavis & Butt-head Show
(1993–   )

One of the most exciting experiences of a typical school day was when one of the budding sociopaths in the class squared off in a showdown with a teacher. Suddenly the drudgerous business of learning stopped while a battle of wills raged between the teacher and the disturbed youngster. We can all still remember the rush of adrenaline watching the drama unfold. Essential to the enjoyment of this moment was the fact that we were spectators, and not actually involved in the confrontation. If you asked any other students not directly involved in the crisis what they thought of the situation, most would immediately admit that the teacher was right.

Even as the thrill of the moment gripped everyone's attention, most of the children realized that the student, being a sapling felon, was as wrong as wrong could be, deserving whatever justice could be meted out. The cold fact is, his classmates would have enjoyed watching the punishment as much as they enjoyed his ill-conceived bravado. Few were ever unsure of who was in the right and who was in the wrong. The excitement of watching in no way meant approval of the young creep's behavior, let alone a temptation to imitate his actions.

So it goes with Beavis and Butt-head. These two "bad boys" meet all the criteria that will most certainly land them in the penal system within a few short years. Two months after experiencing life as the special companions of a larger and even more lethal young felon, the smiles on their faces would be wiped out. This notion constitutes the ultimate fantasy for viewers of this program. If it were announced that they were about to be imprisoned and confronted by others of their ilk, most would be eager to see this episode. We watch this show because we are seeking to bring closure to earlier, unresolved experiences where we were either victimized by such types in school, or we see ourselves as having been like them. In either case, we are all waiting for their deserved beating.

Ben Casey
(1961–66)

Ben Casey is a television program that sounds an alarm bell warning against the dangers of social isolation, and the cruel, unjust worship of America's physicians. Ben is crying out for help, but no one can hear him. A very sad show.

What is wrong with Dr. Casey? His irritable mood continually affects his interpersonal relationships, precipitating chronic social and occupational difficulties. Is it physiological? Might it be that his unforgiving schedule and constant job stress has brought on a sleep disorder? No, it appears to be worse than this. Casey seems incapable of engaging in the routines of intercourse with colleagues and, especially, patients and their families. He is isolated and melancholy and clearly needs help. His fulminating manner intimidates everyone except the kindly Dr. Zorba, a Yoda-like father figure who can reach around Casey's pitiless demeanor. With so many evident symptoms in Dr. Casey, it is curious why Zorba, his supervisor, does not confront him about seeking treatment for his deepening depression. Casey, a cerebral neurosurgeon, plays out a familiar human predicament: The more one becomes absorbed with intellectual matters and detaches from real relationships, the greater the risk of becoming depressed. We can already see the early results in Casey's outbursts of aggression, blunted affect, and deepening social isolation.

Exacerbating the predicament, Casey's profession often shields physicians from getting the help they need. The exalted status of physicians in the American culture has created an image of unapproachability. Physicians are revered in America, becoming an embodiment of the Freudian father-god projection. And it is certainly understandable. Medicine has offered our society a health care system of breathtaking proportions. It seems that there is nothing physicians cannot accomplish. People are rightfully in awe of their expertise and prodigious accomplishments. Physicians give life!

But there is a high price being paid by these masterful, dedicated individuals. We have inadvertently separated and elevated them in a way that injures their personal lives. By subjecting them to the onerous burdens of the social pedestal, we limit their capacity for neediness in relationships. So here is a remarkably gifted clinician who needs relief. But everyone is so awed by his stature that no one approaches him with the love and help he needs—not even his superior and colleague. Et tu, Zorba?

So this program gives one of the first, crucial pinpricks into the inflated balloon of the American high priest, the physician. The deification of the American physician begins to unravel here, and America's physicians are thankful to Ben Casey. It is an unrealistic burden that unfairly props them up beyond their capacity to fulfill people's expectations.

The Brady Bunch
(1969–74)

There are two central, related themes running through this great classic show, one social, the other psychological. It aired in the midst of the Vietnam War during a time when America was a deeply divided nation. For the first time since World War II, there was a deep and growing gulf between generations and ideologies. The polarizing public rhetoric was escalating into social disorder. In response, television gave us *The Brady Bunch*. The theme of the show was har-

mony, blending two families into one. Remember that this was prior to our current, widespread consciousness about the struggle to blend families. The Bradys were pleading with the nation: "Look, if Greg and Marcia can get along, so can all of you! If we will just try, America can be a bunch, just like the Bradys."

The psychological theme is the challenge of bonding with strangers to create intimate family love as siblings. But the complicated challenge here is for the children themselves. On the one hand, they must model how their parents have blended their love, but with the one great exception that forbids stepping over the boundary line into the taboo dimension of lovers. In vivid contrast to their parents, who get to follow through all aspects of their intimate love, the children must repress their strong, adolescent sexual tension and find the delicate balance of sibling closeness. This is a daunting task. The Brady kids, thanks to the stern care of their remarkable parents, did a splendid job!

These two themes are brought together for us as a society as the Bradys to learn the difficult but necessary task of becoming a healthy national family that is close while respecting certain important boundaries. The maturity of the show's vision is reflected in the kids' signature song as they beckon us to not give up, but to "keep on, keep on, keep on, keep on dancing all through the night. . . ." This is an obvious metaphor because the viewer also realizes that the very last thing Carol and Mike would ever allow their children to do would be staying up dancing through the night. The reference is clearly the dance of national harmony. The Brady kids insist that we keep on trying!

Car 54, Where Are You?
(1961–63)

A participatory democracy is a highly fragile organism. Here is a show that offers a ringing call to join the process. Don't leave the exercise of government administration to the unknown. *Car 54* beckons us to mature citizenship; it goads us to vote. Toody and Muldoon are the just deserts of an apathetic citizenry.

There are many television programs that speculate about malevolent civil authority. But think about the quality of your life if public authority was not malevolent, but rather, incompetent? There is a terrifying possibility that those charged with keeping order are inept. The very name of this show raises the unsettling prospect that there could be at least fifty-three other cars occupied by similarly deficient, unskilled simpletons. It represents an American law enforcement nightmare, because we are all at the mercy of the integrity and competence of civil authority. Easing the sting with humor, this show forces us to look at our vulnerability as citizens.

Gunther Toody and Francis Muldoon are drawn in such broad strokes that they really are caricatures. It seems improbable that either of these two first qualified for the rigors of police work and, if so, that their chronic folly would enable them to keep their jobs. Their performance is marginal at best, and frequently amateurish. While they are good men, kind, gentle, and decent, this is clearly not enough.

Confronting the rages of florid antisocial behavior, it is incomprehensible that these two are up to the task. Their vacuous detachment and lumbering affect would sabotage them in the critical situations police officers routinely confront. They would have been dismissed, if they were lucky, and very possibly injured.

Just what is the ideal psychological makeup of an effective law officer? If Toody and Muldoon are the negative extreme, what is the ideal? Although it is tempting to offer platitudes about officers being emotionally in touch and compassionate, there is something to be said for an ability to detach from the grim realities cops actually face. Becoming entangled in emotionally charged situations would soon sap a person of vitality and strength. Individuals with firm personal boundaries, working under the influence and strict discipline of compassionate leadership, is the preferred framework. *Car 54* shows the tragic possibilities when both citizen involvement and administrative leadership deteriorate in democracy. The message here is rather, "Car 55, where are you?"

Dennis the Menace
(1959–63)

A smokescreen suggesting that young Dennis was an incorrigible child, this show is, in fact, not about a bad boy. It is, rather, a show about bad parents. The Mitchells are weak, indecisive, and unable to set appropriate boundaries. As in most of these cases, what is not understood by many parents is that permissiveness is not an excess of kindness. It is rather a cruel form of abandonment.

From our present vantage point, Dennis looks anything but menacing. He seems to be essentially a nice little boy, with perhaps some mild attention deficits. His mischief is so tame by current standards that it is hard to imagine why he is being singled out. However, in the more structured family environment of the fifties, Dennis clearly exhibited conduct problems. He was inappropriately outspoken, especially around adults. His scheming and pranks, mild in our view, were quite precocious in his context.

But all of this misses the point of the show. What must be kept in mind is the larger message. Within the framework of his culture, Dennis was a youngster on the road to problems in adult functioning. Left unchecked, his impertinence would have grown and thereby accelerated consequences for him within the family, with friends and, significantly, in school functioning. It is even possible that Dennis was headed toward problems with the law. As he entered the rebellion of puberty, his acting out was more likely to increase in magnitude and toxicity. His provocations would soon extend beyond the tame bounds of irritating an irascible neighbor. At some point, Dennis inevitably moves from cheeky youngster to flowering sociopath. Where are the exasperated parents then?

No, there is a stern warning here that has sadly been ignored by millions of young parents. The warning is this: "Of course parenting is wearisome! Certainly your children's boundless energy and incessant pressing exhaust you. But there is no option, you simply must endure. It is an act of love. Children need you to set their boundaries because they cannot see the fences on their own. Continuing to give in to their immature, developmentally unformed will has dire consequences for you later. You will regret it for the rest of your life!" Failure to discipline is an act of hostile abandonment. And you will be repaid in kind. Your children will turn on you as young adults, appearing ungrateful after all you have endured. Their adult separation is your just deserts for emotionally separating from them when they needed you to be strong and firm. Indulge your children at your peril! Today's Dennis Mitchell, tomorrow's Eddie Haskell, next year's *America's Most Wanted!* Toughen up, Mom and Dad. Your little "menace" needs your resolute presence.

The Dick Van Dyke Show
(1961–66)

The show demonstrates a series of personality splits that we all relate to at an unconscious level. Tolerating ambivalence, the mixture of good and bad feelings, is a later developmental skill. It is a maturational skill that some never completely master, even into adulthood. The personalities on *The Dick Van Dyke Show* play off these split personality types.

When we are infants, we are unable to comprehend that a person can be both good and bad. They must be one or the other. Mother is experienced alternately as the perfected ideal, and then worthless and abandoning; I love her totally, I am enraged with her. There is no middle ground. Only later does the child learn to hold the good and bad together in one object. This is an important developmental step. *The Dick Van Dyke* program showcased assorted personality dimensions that were paired off against each other.

For instance: Alan Brady and Mel Cooley are the two split-off sides of paternal authority. Alan is irascible and aggressive, frightening as an authority figure; Mel is weak, ineffective, and comedic as an authority figure. This is how the child views the father, alternating between weak and powerful. Sally and Laura are two sides of woman/mother. Laura is weak and dependent and sexually receptive; Sally is strong, independent, a caretaker who is sexually aggressive. Buddy is the other side of Rob. Rob is superego-driven, warm, and connecting; Buddy is self-absorbed, driven, and aggressive. Rob fantasizes being like Buddy; Buddy in his alone times desires to be like Rob.

The show does more than simply present these types. It also favors one over the other. For instance, Alan is definitely preferred over Mel, who is portrayed as a buffoon. Mel Cooley eventually would have snapped. No one can live under a relentless barrage of criticism, ridicule, and humiliating exposure. Mel was the beneficiary of family nepotism, but it came at too high a price. On a daily basis, he is confronted with his incompetence. Since his response is to become rigid and defensive, rather than naturally self-effacing, he is setting himself up for a crisis. Eventually, picture this: Mel on the subway ride to work, dressed in fatigues and a headband; he is nervous and twitching, mumbling to passersby, "what are you looking at?" On that day, God help Alan Brady and Buddy Sorrell!

Don't be fooled by his tough exterior. In fact, Buddy Sorrell is a very sad little man. His upbeat demeanor is mere reaction formation, a compensation for his true feelings about himself. In truth, Buddy feels vulnerable and overwhelmed. His prodigious anger dare not be expressed openly, for fear of parental retaliation. Instead, Buddy must hide behind a shield of misdirected anger through sarcasm and humor. But alone in the night, this iron man weeps in desolation.

Dobie Gillis

(1959–63)

The Gillis family demonstrates a classic scenario for Dobie to have problems later in his life, including an elevated risk for divorce! Careful study of the dynamics between Dobie and his parents can help a young couple assess their own relationship, create healthy distance from their own families, and make a mature decision about their future. This will sharply reduce their own potential for divorce.

Like many families, the Gillises are trying to untangle a complex Oedipal triangle. The show portrays the challenging transition a middle-aged couple confronts as their son emerges into adulthood. Told through the son's eyes, we watch the painful, yet necessary, struggle to redefine each person's role. It exposes both the strengths of their bond, as well as the unhealthy residue of unresolved unconscious issues.

The central character of the show is actually Dobie's mother, Winifred Gillis. She appears somewhat vacuous and detached, but this is just a defense. Although we cannot establish the cause, Mrs. Gillis is, in fact, quite angry. This is seen in the way she manipulates both husband and son, who are engaged in a tug-of-war for her love and attention. Who really owns her affections, Dobie or Dad? Each vies for her love. In the face of her repressed rage, husband Herbert is critical, angry, and immature. A prisoner of his emotions, he is rendered intellectually handcuffed, self-defeating and, of course, impotent in the face of his wife's anger. It is probable that he is reenacting the role he played with his own mother, that of a petulant little boy stamping his feet in impotent defiance.

Dobie's response to his mother's passive domination is displaced in two ways. First, his chronic infatuations with pretty but vapid girls are his transferred attraction to his mother. Any girl who is isolated from her own anger reminds Dobie of Mom and draws him like a magnet. He is turned off by Zelda, the available, loving girl who is too connected to her feelings. Zelda expresses herself too directly for Dobie's comfort. Second, Dobie unconsciously retaliates against his parents by associating with Maynard Krebs. Balancing Dobie, the anal-retentive, clean man, is Maynard, the anal-intensive, soiled man. Dobie's unspoken threat is that he, too, will become dirty, dependent, and shameful.

In the knotty web at home, Mom does not adequately shield Dobie from Dad's anger. In fact, she uses his anger to retaliate against Dobie. For one thing, his constant dreaming is a painful reminder of the prison into which she has sentenced herself. Here she is, living out the treasure of her life in the stifling, cultural dust bowl of a small town grocery store, eking out a marginal living with a man-child husband. To make matters worse, she is being abandoned, left behind by her loving, child-man son! How unfair! His life holds out the promise of freedom while she remains incarcerated. No wonder she is so angry.

Father Knows Best
(1954–63)

If father is so wonderful, why is his son so angry? While life seems fine for Mom, Dad, and the girls, there is definitely something amiss with young Bud Anderson. Behind their veneer of middle-class perfection, might there be something terribly wrong in this family? Could it be something organic with the boy? The show never clarifies the issue, and we are left to imagine what became of Bud in later life. All the signs were there for significant problems for both Bud and the Anderson family.

There is a feel to Bud that emanates through the screen. It seems subtle at first, but there is an unmistakably dark quality to him. It is perhaps most apparent in his judgment of other people and situations. He seems to wander into trouble, and his manner of communicating is at times sneeringly provocative. On the surface his manners appear to be fine. After all, he was well taught at home. However, there is a devious quality that makes it apparent to everyone else who encounters him that this boy cannot be trusted. He is constantly choosing the wrong companions, making the wrong decisions, and having to confess and repent later to his parents and the others he has offended. But despite the hopeful tone of the mood music in the background, the viewer is not encouraged that this will be Bud's final, lasting repentance. We just know that there is plenty more psychodrama ahead for him.

Bud is not an overtly unlikable adolescent. He is not an Eddie Haskell type. There is no ostentatious politeness masking a bitter contempt for adults. Eddie is clearly angry with his parents and retaliates against all adults, especially the Cleavers. In his case, it appears to be simple jealousy for the love and attention that he is missing in his own home. But there is a deeper problem with the Anderson boy. He appears to be holding something inside. We will never know what is really going on, but there are other dimensions to this family that are not seen in public. One clue is found in the manner in which father and son interact. Unlike Ward Cleaver, the other classic 1950s father, Jim is angry and impatient with his son. He often thinks the worst of him and is ready to believe that Bud is involved in some mischief. So Bud is playing the part of the deviant his father expects of him.

Millions of people can identify with family secrets. There is a mask presented to the outside world. Often even the extended family is unaware that there are toxic dynamics at work. Everything appears to be normal and healthy. But inside the intimacies of family life, there is unbridled anger and abusive manipulations alive and at work. There is no compelling evidence that the Andersons are anything but an emotionally open, loving, and healthy family. But there is this matter of Bud and his unctuous personality. The family might be

blind to it, but here in their midst is a flowering personality disorder destined to rebel in dramatic and flamboyant ways as a late teen. If and when that happens, will the Andersons be truly shocked? Will Betty and Kathy understand it? Did they see it coming, too? We will never know.

The Flying Nun
(1967–70)

The premise here is not some mindless fantasy trip about a gifted nun who defies the laws of physics. This show is actually a provocative lesson about personal power. In vivid contrast to shows like *Batman* and *Superman,* here we have a very different kind of statement about power. This show says to us, if you will stop resisting the environment, if you will only attune yourself to nature, to the direction and flow of the world's winds, you too can fly! Sister Bertrille is saying: Look at me! I am a frail little creature, humble and silly. Yet I can soar above you with the turn of my veil.

As farfetched as all this may sound, I can assure you that there is valid scientific basis for this view. In fact, the University of Iowa conducted an interesting study

in 1983. The researchers took two groups of laboratory rats. One group was taught to utilize meditation and yoga techniques. In essence, these rats were conditioned to being spiritually centered and quiescent. The other group was given no such conditioning. They then fixed onto the heads of all these rats a Flying Nun-like habit, a tiny replica of the headpiece that Sister Bertrille wore on the show. They then took the rats and pushed them off a cliff. Remarkably, the group without the conditioning fell directly to the ground, many of them suffering cramping and sprained knees. In contrast, every one of the spiritual rats actually began to soar on the wind drafts. So there we have it. Tell me, just where is the boundary between real life and television?

Frasier
(1994–   )

This show is about father rage, centering around two brothers, Frasier and Niles Crane, who are the offspring of an uneducated, gruff, even crude, blue-collar worker. Yet both Frasier and his brother Niles grew to be sophisticated, erudite, effete, urbane, academic snobs. How in the world did this happen? What was going on in their childhood that they felt they had to so dramatically distance themselves from even the slightest characteristic of their father's. They are, in essence, the opposite of their father. The most intriguing question is, what in the name of heaven was mother like?

Think about your own personality. Take out a clean sheet of paper and make a list of your personal characteristics. Write down as many as you can. Completely catalogue your characteristics. When you have made as exhaustive a list as possible, take another clean sheet of paper and do the same thing for each of your parents. List all of their personality characteristics as best you can. Ask them questions when you are unsure. While there may be certain dimensions about their private life that might escape you, in general, you are well aware of what they were like.

Now compare your list with theirs. Which parent are you most like? With whom have you identified? What habits have you cultivated that are like, or strikingly unlike, your mother or father? If you are adopted, research your birth parents and learn what you can about their personal habits and television interests. If

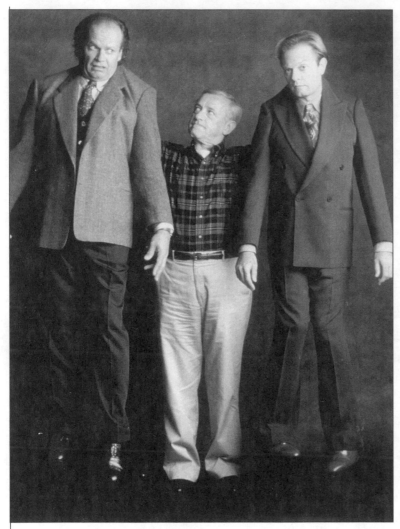

you cannot do this, the process will work just fine with your adoptive parents or any primary caretaker. If, like Frasier and Niles, you have dramatically differentiated yourself from one or both of your parents, you must ask yourself why. What is it that caused you to take such elaborate steps away from them. What has been the impact on your life?

In the case of the Crane boys, imagine how much ridicule they endured their entire lives at the hands of their, more than likely, blue-collar extended family. It must be unbearable at family weddings, picnics, or other gatherings. Imagine a typical scene at a niece's wedding. Frasier and Niles are cornered by their crude uncle who, speaking with his mouth full of food, proceeds to regale them with a highly detailed account of a doctor's visit to have a sensitively located boil lanced. As the two refined siblings struggle to quell the nausea, one wonders, why choose this path of misery? It would have seemed more logical for Frasier and Niles to be seen belly laughing at this same story as the true peers of their blood relative. There they are, dressed in garish blue rented tuxedoes with black felt shoes, drinking whiskey and ginger ale, which they spill freely on their shirts. This was actually their destiny. What psychologically intense experience jarred them into the entirely incongruous life they now lead? It demonstrates the raw transforming power of the unconscious! All of this could have been avoided if only Frasier and Niles had paid more attention to the lessons before them as young boys as they watched *Dobie Gillis* and *The Waltons*. In each of those shows, the universal struggle of a young man to create his own identity in the face of a strong father would have given them some less radical strategies than the one they chose.

What is important is that you do not make the same mistake! Frasier and Niles suffer identity problems, but you can watch them and avoid the same self-destructive path. It should be quite clear to you now: Frasier teaches and heals!

Gomer Pyle, U.S.M.C.
(1964–70)

This show is a statement about the limitations of intellectual wisdom as a path to psychological and spiritual contentment. It also observed that stupidity is often less an involuntary handicap than an unconscious, defensive choice serving to keep us safely unaware in a dangerous world.

Here is a man of innocence, filled with apparent goodness, but lacking cultivation. Gomer is unsophisticated, appears to have minimal intellectual capacity, and is without guile. He is a simpleton who ruins almost every task assigned to him. While humorous to some degree, the reality is that Gomer refuses to be accountable for his responsibilities. A consistent bungler, he forces the system to work around his ineptitude. He perpetually frustrates those around him, especially his superiors.

Volatile Sergeant Vince Carter has scarce tolerance for Gomer. He rightly senses that there is something false and manipulative about Gomer's famed inadequacy. Repeated acts of witless behavior infuriate Carter who, not being psychologically minded, is baffled by Pyle's incapacity to use his intellectual ability. Why would a grown man so persistently refuse to become mentally focused? Why indeed? He knows Gomer can do more and better. He suspects that Gomer, behind his shield of naive innocence, is actually someone who unconsciously chooses to fail. And this is not acceptable. In any event, spending five years as a private is certainly an indication of a self-defeating personality disorder.

Carter always refers to Gomer simply as "Pyle." The sound of the name is

telling. Actually he is calling him "Pile." Pile of what? This obvious dung reference is meant to convey Carter's contempt. It reflects Carter's awareness that Gomer is a useless pile since he refuses to utilize his true capacity. A person who will not flourish as a rational, thinking being is not truly human. He is an imitation, a pile of waste.

But the show has even more to say. Being content is not related to one's intelligence. The uneducated want the privileged class to know that goodness is not their exclusive domain. You can be wise and still full of evil. Gomer calls to us to live a simpler life, with fewer complications. Achievement is an overrated virtue. Better to remain at the bottom of the social ladder if the choice of advancement is losing your soul. Gomer confronts Carter's apoplectic, ulcerous lifestyle with a peaceful alternative. Who's to say which is better?

Green Acres
(1965–71)

What do we make of this couple who claims that their relocation to the country was planned and anticipated, but who so consistently fail to accomplish even the rudiments of sociocultural adaptation. Either there is some undisclosed trauma that triggers their move, or else, sadly, they are completely detached from reality. If it is the latter, then this is a psychotic couple who will soon be hospitalized against their will. But I think there is something else going on with the Douglas family.

This show offers the inverse of *The Beverly Hillbillies* premise. They share a fundamental similarity. There is something ill advised about their move. Both families would have been better served remaining in their home town and, if necessary, seeking treatment at a local mental health clinic. Their relocation is precipitous, poorly planned, and exacerbates problems rather than solving them. In the case of the Douglases, however, their move is especially reckless. It raises clinical suspicions about the mental health of this couple. There is a disorder where individuals suddenly and unexpectedly travel away from home and assume a new identity. Is that what we are seeing here, a dual psychogenic fugue? Let's consider.

The Douglas couple would have us believe that they voluntarily relocated from New York City to the rural Midwest. This assertion is not credible. Not that they were coerced by any outside force, but it is more likely that their move was triggered by some psychological factor, which impelled them to radically disrupt their life. At their age, and given their life experience and evident success, a decision to dislocate themselves in such a extreme manner would clearly be a carefully planned, well anticipated event. Their change in lifestyle would have been welcomed and anticipated. For instance, they would have achieved more agreement between them as a couple. And they surely would have conducted a thorough investigation into their new home town and its people. But this is not so.

In fact, what is crystal clear is that this late middle-aged couple has failed to fully inculturate into their new, sought after, rural home. They have physically moved, but they have not psychologically relocated. They even dress as if they are back in the city. For someone who claims to have longed for country life for a long time, Oliver seems ill suited to the rigors of country life. In particular, he has little tolerance for the peculiarities of the local people. Why is he surprised and frustrated by the Mr. Haneys and the Eb Dawsons? Who did he expect to find in Hooterville? Had he never visited before? What is going on here?

There might have been some trauma that occurred with the Douglases that is never disclosed. They are fleeing New York to what they fantasize will be a better place. The part of the fool in this drama is played by Arnold Ziffel, the town pig. He is teaching the Douglases some crucial facts of life. This grimy little animal parades around in front of them as if to say, "You may think that you don't fit here, that you are losing the battle of inculturation. But in fact, it is no different here in Hooterville than in your beloved New York. Every place has its soiled reality. The alleged glamour and sophistication of your precious urban environment has the swine of poverty and crime parading through your living room as well. Give up the fight and settle in a new sty." Arnold Ziffel confronts them with their insanity, and they don't see it. The Douglases are in need of professional help.

Gunsmoke
(1955–75)

We often fail to adequately anticipate the consequences of our actions. Here we look at the issue of how we face the music for an action already completed. The gun is smoking! The bullet has already left, and you cannot retrieve it. The deed is done. What will you do now? Matt Dillon, a healthy, integrated man, is here to help you sort it all through.

The immature response to error is to fantasize that we can return and nullify the occurrence. *Gunsmoke* presents us the mature alternative: Face the reality, prepare for repercussions, accept appropriate consequences, and learn for your further growth. The name bespeaks a unique predicament in the human condition. What do we do in the moment when the gun is already smoking? The deed is done, the act is finished. Prevention is no longer relevant. It is now time for the consequences. How do you go on with your life after the bullet is already spent? For too many of us, the norm is impulsive reaction. But *Gunsmoke* patiently counsels action, not reaction. It even extended itself from thirty to a full sixty minutes to better enable Marshal Dillon to help us in our search for rationality.

The heart of the show was the confrontation between Marshal Dillon and some outlaw. It was typically an individual set on a tragic course who felt he could not back down without losing face. This pride became a veritable suicide gesture. The deficiency of such a gesture is repeated every week for the viewer in order to help us recondition our own judgment in the middle of crisis. The lesson is that there is never a "point of no return." Such stubbornness is mere hubris. It is self-destructive, and you will certainly face the music. You will face the estimable Marshal Matt Dillon. And you will surely end up buried on Boot Hill. Good-bye, my foolish friend.

The real tragedy is that this alternative is always unnecessary. Matt Dillon is a solid, mature, integrated individual. He is in touch with his feelings, his feminine side, and is ready to become emotionally close in relationships. He is beloved in the town. He is surrounded by others whose lives he helped salvage, among them Kitty Russell, a depressed saloon owner, and Chester, his melancholy deputy with the pronounced gait abnormality. Dillon is a role model for good authority. He always prefers the peaceful remedy to violence. But he also has no difficulty fulfilling his official obligations to the law. Buttressed by the authority of the community, Dillon understands that strict enforcement of law cannot be abrogated. But if we will stop the trigger of reaction after the first bullet has left the chamber, we have a chance. Dillon appeals to us: Put down the gun and let's reason this out together. There will be consequences, but they will not be as bad as they will if you continue your present course. Please!

The Honeymooners
(1955–71)

Depicting the sad state of the postindustrial, American male, Ralph Kramden is a man in intense emotional pain, regressed, and out of control. The consequences of this pervasive character pathology include not only an individual man's marginal functioning but, tragically, the victimization of women as well. Ralph is crying out for help on behalf of millions of American men. And Alice is, too.

What does the therapist see when Ralph Kramden comes for treatment? When a complete picture of his functioning emerges in the assessment, what does the clinician suspect is wrong with Mr. Kramden? Surely there is something wrong.

There is certainly evidence of a chronic eating disorder. This might be hormonal, but other behavior patterns suggest a psychosomatic etiology. It would be interesting to know if Ralph had attendant gastrointestinal problems or high blood pressure. A complete physical examination is clearly the first step.

Beyond physiological complications, Ralph shows many symptoms of a disturbed personality. His volcanic anger might indicate a histrionic or borderline personality disorder. Perhaps this is an Intermittent Explosive Disorder. What fuels his rage? Was it alcohol or other drugs? Did an early trauma precipitate his high-voltage defense? Was he the child of a disturbed personality, an addict, or both? In addition, Ralph is prone to episodes of grandiosity, raising suspicions of mania, narcissism, or even simple caffeine intoxication. It is highly probable that he struggled with anxiety-based, sexual difficulties. All in all, not a pretty picture.

There is another perspective here that is more sociological than psychological.

Surely Ralph had psychological problems needing attention. But in some ways the show is less about a disturbed individual man, than it is an allegory about a socially and psychologically disturbed group of men. Ralph typifies the dilemma of many American husbands. Missing key pieces of his developmental puzzle, Ralph is regressed and still needing basic nurturing. Yet his very defensive makeup mitigates against getting the suckle he desperately needs.

Even the theatrical movement of the show emphasizes Ralph's quandary. Alice is forever having to leave the room, and is absent for long periods of the drama. Ralph repeatedly pushes her out of the scene because his neediness is only expressed in brutal, distancing ways. Alice desires to love Ralph and be near him, but she must continually flee from his infantile fury. So he destroys the very opportunity he craves. Needing emotional closeness, his very manner of expressing this need pushes his wife away. What a tragedy! Yet it tells the tale for millions of American husbands, sinking into a vortex of self-defeating isolation. Ralph Kramden would eventually push Alice completely out of his life. Before long even Ed and Trixie Norton might overcome their codependent propensities and also abandon Ralph. Without help, Ralph Kramden's future looks rather desolate.

I Love Lucy
(1951–61)

Lucy made a case for the urgent need to rescue women from the shackles of male patriarchy in the traditional American marriage. It forecast the coming feminist revolution that would be in high gear twenty years later. Lucy Ricardo was a pioneer in the face of significant odds.

Arguably the most dominant television program in history, this snapshot of American values in the 1950s has endured as a valued relic in our culture. The Ricardos were simultaneously typical and unique as an American family. On the one hand, they depicted a standard for the role of men and women in marriage in the postwar period. Like most, this family was male dominated. In fact, for dramatic emphasis, the male role was played by Ricky Ricardo, a Latin man, serving to emphasize machismo and strong male identity. In such a typical American patriarchy, albeit benevolent, the man dominates the woman. The show depicts Lucy's ongoing struggle to shake off this benevolent male dominance.

Lucy's aspiration was to succeed in show business. This is an accepted fantasy for every American. Becoming a star is the shallow, narcissistic American image of becoming a fully actualized self. Lucy was always wanting to use her husband's influence to advance her career, but he consistently refused. Although Lucy is bright and capable, all of her efforts fail, and many end in catastrophe and painful futility. The message here is clear: "If you try to rise above your appropriate station, dear woman, you will always end up in trouble and need to be extricated by a man. So do not attempt to move up and out of your assigned role. If you try, the consequences to you will be emotionally devastating. Remember your humiliating experience in the chocolate factory? Please, stay home or you will end up badly. It is where you belong, in service to the man. Allow the man to take care of your needs. I will go out into the world with the power. Your power is not suited for leadership, but for service. This is what God wants for you."

Well thank God for Lucy's indomitable spirit! Lucy shook off this stultifying role and determined to become her full self. She inspired not only Ethel, her socially anesthetized disciple, but millions of other women as well. Perhaps Lucy's energy and commitment forecast what would later become a full gender eruption in America. And she did this in the face of very difficult odds. After all, the Ricardos were also a unique family. Remember that Lucy married a Latin man. Given the social climate of the country, both she and Ricky and, painfully, her young son, were almost certainly subjected to the ugly realities of racial prejudice. Perhaps this explains her frenetic, anxiety-fueled pace and energy, almost a mania at times. Was this a constructive compensation for the sadness and anger she must have felt? How many viewers connected with her around this unconscious issue? How many viewing women themselves felt imprisoned by men and so reveled in a vicarious identification with Lucy's schemes to escape her imprisonment?

Leave It to Beaver
(1957–63)

A glimpse into the early dynamics shaping baby boomer beliefs, this show depicts the last gasp of the modern American value system. These are convictions Ward defined, June obeyed, Wally idealized and, sadly, Beaver struggled to achieve. Beaver announces to America: "Get ready for my postmodern world." It provides an early forecast of the Clinton Presidency.

Theodore "Beaver" Cleaver is, in many ways, a sad little boy. A doughty, ne'er-do-well little oaf, he is victimized by having a sibling of enormous potential. Not that Wally is a prodigy, but he is a young man who embodies every ideal his father and American, postwar, middle-class culture lionize. He is handsome, athletic, articulate, and full of charisma. Beaver is pudgy, clumsy, and tongue-tied. When the show ends, he is just entering puberty. As he struggles to separate from his parents, their obvious partiality for Wally will become clear to him. At this point, Beaver will begin to get in touch with his deep anger.

Beaver is the type to hold it inside, repressed. He was not likely to rebel in a dramatic, antisocial manner. He is more likely to become passively enraged, i.e., depressed. Beaver is the type to remain frozen in adolescence, continuing to be involved in activities well beyond their appropriate time. He might keep a paper route until he is seventeen and remain in the Boy Scouts after high school. As part of his unconscious retaliation against his parents, Beaver might live at home with them into his late twenties. He would infuriate Ward and June with poor academic achievement, slothful behavior, sloppy personal habits, and perhaps even dramatic weight gain. His hostile passivity, sluggish negligence, and gnawing presence would heap hot coals of punishment on Ward and June. Like his nickname, Beaver would gnaw away at the legs of his parents' marriage until it fell like a chewed oak. Rather than leaving to attend "State" like Wally, he would more likely attend a local college, taking six years to finish his bachelor's degree. Beaver would be the first in the family to experiment with drugs, protest the war, pursue an immature marriage, get divorced, and enter therapy in his thirties to alleviate his eroding, depressive anger.

One of the blessings for Beaver would be the social eruption of the late 1960s. From his perspective, thank God for Vietnam and the social cataclysm it ignited. In many ways it would save the Beaver. This event would serve to raise doubts about, and ultimately discredit, many of the value norms that constricted Beaver as a young man. Much of what Wally saluted would be called into question. Beaver's sympathy for the antiwar movement would enrage his father and buttress Beaver's own self-esteem.

For their part, Ward and June typify white, suburban, middle-class, postwar Americans. June, forced into a life of home-bound servitude, might be struggling against a low-grade depression. But Ward is far more repressed than June, who is more likely just culturally compliant. She is devoted to her family relationships, but dependent on her husband and thus economically enslaved. June is keenly poised to hear the feminist call to emerge to power on her own terms. She probably would return to her own career and thus shed the weighty blanket of a smothering patriarchy. She might very well join the women's movement and go back to college. It would be interesting to watch Ward's reaction. Just how brittle is he?

Eddie Haskell, one of the most memorable people from the show, might very well develop a personality disorder in adult life. He certainly struggles with his conduct as a child and adolescent. He is devious, manipulative, and less aware of the feelings of others. Eddie would have problems in occupational and social functioning. At best, he would become someone who repeatedly tangled with coworkers, causing strife on the job, thereby thwarting his own success, a self-defeating personality. At worst, he might deteriorate into a petty criminal or, in a massive reaction formation, become a police officer or a crossing guard.

Yes, the Cleavers were a family in deep trouble.

Mister Ed
(1961–65)

Mister Ed teaches us lessons both intimate and grand. Through this show we can gain insight into ourselves as individuals and our place in the community of species in the cosmos. Who are we and where are we in the order of creation? Ed offers incisive, important commentary on the human condition.

Mister Ed offers us a fascinating metaphor on a fundamental human dynamic. The idea of a talking horse appears at first glance to be rather frivolous, but there is more here than meets the eye. *Mister Ed* has much to teach us. The show depicts the struggle between our mental life and our base instincts. As a horse, Ed represents our raw instinctual power, our sexuality. After all, the horse is the animal that looks the most naked. There is an animal in each of us. It is this part of us that needs to be controlled, corralled, if you will. So Ed is the projected embodiment of Wilbur's sexual self. In service to the show's purpose, Wilbur is depicted as a man devoid of sexuality. His sexuality has unconsciously been put into Ed who, in fact, on the surface has personality traits similar to Wilbur's own. Ed reflects Wilbur's uncertainty about his power. Feeling uncomfortable with his natural inclinations to race through a meadow, Ed reads and engages in intellectual pursuits, a defense against his discomfort with his body. Ed depicts the human challenge: We must ensure that our intellect remains in charge of our animal power or, like Ed's nonspeaking brothers and sisters, we would break loose and run wild across the range. This we can never tolerate in ourselves.

Beyond this, Ed offers us an important perspective in our search to understand the place of humanity in the larger creation. If a horse, or any so-called lower animal form, had cognitive capacity, would they too sublimate their drives and build a complex, equinian civilization? *Mister Ed* says, "Don't be so arrogant about your perceived superior role in nature." Imagine what we, the horses, would do. Imagine a planet dominated by the horse perspective. Imagine horse art. Imagine horses subjugating other species for their own purposes. Enslaving humans, perhaps. Driving to a street corner, two horses stop and notice a horse selling velvet paintings of humans playing poker. "How tacky!" they observe, and drive on. *Mister Ed* says, "There but for the grace of God, go you!"

The Munsters
(1964–66)

People who are socially isolated because they are different become monsters. The Munsters are a family of physically challenged individuals who desire to fit in, but are prevented from doing so. It is a statement about the cruelty that results from ordinary human terror of the unknown. Other people become victims because we cannot adequately address our fears. The Munsters are tragic victims of such

social rigidity. They were forced to carve out a bubble of their own reality in order to shield themselves from the cruelties of the world.

An American, middle-class version of the Frankenstein fable, the television Munster family more fully embellishes the Mary Shelley vision. The lesson of Frankenstein is that, if you are different, people will want to separate from you. As a result, if you are socially shunned and isolated, you will indeed become a monster. It becomes a self-fulfilling prophecy. However, when people come to know who you are, when they invest in the complications of a close relationship with you, then surely you will become beautiful to them. It is axiomatic. As viewers, we have come to know this family: Herman, Lily, Eddie, and Grandpa. Certainly we are aware of their uniqueness and eccentricities. But we are not afraid of them; nor are we put off by them. We enjoy who they are, and appreciate their loving, kind way.

Beautiful niece Marilyn is actually considered ugly by the family and has their sympathy for being so unattractive. This is obviously a diversion, a defense against the bitter pain of their own social rejection. Here is an entire family of physically challenged individuals turning the tables and seeing Marilyn as handicapped! It offers clear evidence that normalcy is entirely contextual. Within the sociocultural setting of the Munster family, Marilyn is indeed abnormal. This raises an interesting point. If it were the case that the rest of the community resembled the Munsters, their view of Marilyn is rational. However, for them not to see that it is they, not Marilyn, who are different, speaks to their psychological detachment. This is a family with faulty reality testing. And why? Because it is a coping mechanism for them. If they remain oblivious to their own oddity, they can function within the brutal environment of social pressure. Surely they are under great stress for their appearance and manner. So to blot it out and act as though they were the normal ones is testimony to the power of projection, denial, and repression, among other psychological defenses.

My Three Sons
(1960–72)

This show postulates the feasibility of the all male family. It basically asks the question: "Does a family really need women? Other than for conception, are they truly necessary for a healthy family environment? Can a full-fledged patriarchy work?" But this experiment is made in the midst of very painful circumstances.

The Douglases were not hostile to women by any means. The show does not negate or reject women. It simply probes the possibilities. Should circumstances unfold that a group of men find themselves gathered in a family, can they flourish in an all male environment? Must they seek out women to remain healthy? To its credit, the show answers yes. Family health is optimal when it is gender balanced as well as age and dependency balanced. But this was not so at the beginning.

As a father, it must be remembered that Steve Douglas was a grieving widower.

He had suffered the loss of his wife, friend, and mother of their three boys. Being a typical, white, middle-class male in the American culture of the 1960s, it is highly probable that he found it difficult to connect with his deep feelings of loss and abandonment. The notion of being angry at his dead wife would be a horrible thought to him, thus condemning him to a prolonged repressive suffering. This most certainly explains his emotional distance as a father. There is no doubt that he loved the boys, but there are consequences when a person fails to complete the process of grieving. Steve lived in an era that predated much of what is known today about the more helpful ways to recover from the devastation of losing a spouse.

So Steve struggles along with his grief intact. He sets out, unconsciously, to carry on without a woman. To accentuate this, he brings in his father-in-law, Bub O'Casey to fill in for his dead wife. Bub takes over the cooking, cleaning, house maintenance, and other traditionally, unmistakable female functions. The boys' new mother is a salty old man. How reactionary can this be? "If women can't be trusted to stay around, then I'll get a man to be our woman!" Even when Bub leaves a few years later, he is replaced by yet another man, Bub's crusty old brother, Steve's Uncle Charley. These two caretakers, while good men and full of love, are the most masculine of men. Each is like an old sailor, barking their nurturing through stern orders and admonitions. This is "Helga" mothering, a testosterone breast. The boys obey and Steve carries on in isolation. Left to him, there might have been yet another generation of roughneck mothering for the family. Who knows how many stout old uncles there are in the family?

Attempts by the boys to thaw the environment are at first unwelcome. No sooner does oldest son Mike become serious with girlfriend Sally, then he disappears from the family. Off and married, we never hear from him again. In fact, he is promptly replaced by the adopted Ernie, curiously a nerd who is much less seductive than Mike. He probably was given Mike's room, old clothes, and inheritance. There is a cold chill in the Douglas home. Finally in 1966, through the efforts of son Robbie, the first woman is allowed to come in and stay with the family. She dutifully takes her place as a demure lady, obsequious to Charley's role as woman of the house, and endears herself forever by promptly giving birth to triplet boys! This miracle is nothing short of an act of God. It is the breakthrough that Steve's wounded heart needs. In the aftermath of this event, Steve himself relents and reaches out to Barbara, Ernie's teacher and warm mother figure. With this, the healing is complete, and the Douglas family's long, stormy recovery breaks. One can only hope that Steve eventually reached out to recover his lost son Mike.

The Partridge Family
(1970–74)

This show fuses two powerful American fantasies of the sixties and seventies. During these turbulent times, most American youth were conditioned by social teaching that the happiest, most fulfilled life was one characterized by a strong family system. But the wider popular culture was also conveying another message. The ideal dream for every young person was the fame, riches, and adulation associated with being a rock 'n' roll singing star. The most sought after goal of every young American was to be the next rock idol.

Central to these two ideals, family and rock stardom, was their apparent incompatibility. Being a rock star was alien to family life, and a strong family life was not the path to rock stardom. But in this show, *The Partridge Family* says "nonsense!" They embody the twin ideals together. They say to us, "You can have a strong family and rock star success. It is possible! It may be difficult, but this is America and anything is possible. Look at us. Not only does Mom cook for the band, Mom is in the band!" *The Partridge Family,* a depiction of the perfect American life.

The Patty Duke Show
(1963–66)

A teaching fable, this portrait of two identical cousins is in fact about the struggle to merge a split identity into one whole, mature person. More a deep dream reality than a depiction of waking reality, Patty and Cathy are playing out the universal struggle for identity. The happy ending is not sibling peace, but a finished, cohesive blending of these two different dimensions of one young girl.

At what point in the life of a young adult does natural immaturity move into the realm of character disturbance? This is Patty Lane's predicament. Teenagers Patty and Cathy are in the midst of late adolescent turmoil. Their full selves are emerging. In this television allegory, there is actually only one person, with two competing dimensions. A mighty internal battle is underway to determine which core identity would dominate. Would it be Patty, Cathy or, God help her, both?

Each of us has an inner sense that there is more than one dimension to our personality. We show one dimension to the public and withhold another for ourselves and our intimates. This is normal, except when they feel too split off from one another and begin to feel like entirely separate entities. Is this what was going on with Patty and Cathy? It is a sign of maturity that we no longer feel a need to guard ourselves with others. When we finally shed adolescent anxiety, we become secure in presenting our authentic self to the world. Some people take many years into adulthood to accomplish this process. For some, they forge a compromise that never fully integrates their diverse feelings. These are the individuals who later become troubled.

As young, growing people, it is natural that we take pains to show others our best self, our ideal image: cultured, educated, integrated. This is our "Cathy Within."

This is the part of us that seeks to bond in relationships. We also have an aggressive dimension. We can be critical, angry, and disorganized. This is the "Patty Within." It is this unguarded affect that our intimates see. Maturity is when the various dimensions fuse together, and we no longer feel any splits inside. We are comfortable with who we are and spontaneously show this to the world. So we are less the Patty or Cathy at a given moment. Rather, we are reconnected and become one again. The tension in this show is that the two sides confront each other in a battle for dominance. The final outcome is uncertain. There is a feeling that each secretly wants the other to win. Who would you like to see dominate? The answer says a lot about you.

Perry Mason
(1957–74)

We all have a deep desire to be rescued by a strong, loving, capable father. Of particular interest here is that this show reflects that sentiment from a very early, preverbal stage of our development.

Who helps us when we are wrongly accused, when all the evidence incriminates us? Who stands up for us when we are indicted by the great prosecutor? In the complex infant triangle, negotiating our way through the relational maze with goddess-Mommy and god-Daddy, we are often caught between them. Given the disparity of power, this is experienced as a terrifying predicament. As our social education begins, we experience the painful connection of our behavior and their approval and disapproval. In the unfolding drama of childhood discipline, we learn the intricacies of manipulating one parent against the other. Memories of this early psychodrama are the marrow of our fascination with *Perry Mason*.

Perry plays the omnipotent father-defender who can confront the prosecutor-mother. He enters as a powerful advocate, nearly equal to mother in raw power and crafty enough to match wits with her. He comes in and saves us from final conviction and the death sentence. In this tragicomedy, mother is analogous to the public authorities. She is the overseeing caretaker, responsible for peace and rules enforcement in the home jurisdiction. We have been confronted with damning evidence of a wrongdoing. Our lame protestations are as futile as they are feeble.

The essence of our problem is that we don't have the proper words; we are unable to speak for ourselves. When we are young children, we are inarticulate and no match for mother's superb verbal skills. So we cannot declare our innocence with credibility. Ah, but father is her match and more! He will come in and, using his own great words, will vindicate us before mother, the judge, and the jury. This is a grand symbol of the reverence we hold for the powers of our parents. How sad adults lose touch with the frightening width of this chasm for little children.

Perry understands the ramification here. He is a devoted advocate for those caught in the vice, facing against a good, but unknowing authority. He will not fail us. His physique and even his name, Mason, indicate strength, immovability. He is a concrete man, a warrior with a stone constitution. He will not be dissuaded, and he will not crumble before Mother as we are sure to do!

The Rifleman
(1958–63)

A young boy's Oedipal nightmare, the Rifleman is a brooding, aggressive father with an ominous tendency to flaunt his prodigious instrument of death, an obvious penis substitute, his special rifle. Poor Mark is at the mercy of a father who loves him but reminds him of the futility of ever trying to measure up in competition with this man. Imagine if your own father was a Goliath who boasted of his mastery with the slingshot. My God, what hope is left for this young boy?

Lucas McCain is a wounded man. A widower with limited affective resources, he is emotionally constricted in the face of a great grief. "My dear wife is gone! What to do with this pain? To make matters worse, I am left with this little boy who is needy, and yet who's face is the very vision of my beloved, dead wife. It is almost unbearable to look at him." What a psychological conflict: to dearly love the son, who is a constant reminder of a ghastly loss. You can feel McCain's ambivalence when you watch the two together. Lucas loves Mark, but keeps his distance. There is a strong feeling of impatient anger in his disciplining. Certainly Mark is afraid of him. You can almost see him flinch when his Paw raises his hand. Yet Paw does love this boy, made of the stuff of his very own self.

It is no wonder Lucas finds solace in the power of his extraordinary rifle. A custom-made .44 Winchester rifle, it is a mighty instrument. McCain wields it as if it were an extension of his own body. Leveled at the waist, he rapid fires and is always the last man standing in the face of the rival. Even Sheriff Micah, the protecting authority, defers to the bigger weapon. He knows he is no match for the McCain instrument. So the entire community feels protected by this grieving man's displaced anger. Thank God for his own strong ego boundaries. Lucas struggles with his anger but, in the end, he always knows which way to point the rifle.

Our sincere hope is that Lucas will resolve his anger before Mark begins his teenage separation from father. If Lucas resists this healthy boundary testing by his son, continuing to dominate and cower him, it will have injurious consequences for Mark's maturation. Worse, it might damage this loving relationship between father and son. If he unwittingly allows this to happen, Lucas will lose his son as well. Then he will be truly alone. God help lawbreakers if this occurs. McCain's rifle will be white hot with use. There will be rivers of blood flowing in North Fork, New Mexico.

The Twilight Zone
(1959–64)

Rod Serling takes us on a visit to an unresolvable infant terror: the death fear. By scaring us into a profound anxiety state, reminiscent of the very feelings we had in our crib, Rod helps us to exercise our skills of repression. This ability is crucial to adult functioning. We must learn to ignore the uncontrollable environment's dangers that would otherwise immobilize us. This is a wonderful gift.

As infants, we are unrepressed; we do not unconsciously choose to shut out unpleasant reality. In fact, babies are on full alert to reality, trying to comprehend and sort everything that confronts them. Utterly dependent and completely vulnerable, they live at the mercy of external forces. Thank God for Mother! The memory of this infantile terror never fully leaves us. We are constantly trying to overcome our primordial vulnerability. Later, when we develop the capacity for repression, we use it to protect ourselves from the consequences of a tidal wave of overwhelming reality. It is ever present in our unconscious experience, repressed from awareness so that we can function with confidence.

155

All this gives a clue to the fascination we have as adults with horror stories. By revisiting the original feeling of fear, we hope to conquer once and for all an uncontrollable environment. Serling is a master of manipulating these feelings. Through his tales, Rod helps you reconnect to that frightening period in your life and reminds you just how vulnerable you are in this world. But there is one big difference between the adult and infant experience. At the end of a horror tale, there is a resolution that reaffirms your own security and survival. Sometimes it comes within the story itself, as when the protagonist survives the danger. Other times, even in the face of the hero's demise, the story ends and we are temporarily healed by the awareness that it was just fiction, not real life. Thus we are able to disconnect from these frightening unconscious thoughts and feelings and resume "normal" functioning.

So Rod helps us regain perspective. He says "boo!" but reminds us that we can turn on the lights at any time and make the monster disappear. Don't be afraid; you will be all right; there's really nothing there. Scary stories reconnect you to your inner child, the one who was hyper-aware of the environment's killing dangers. For the time you are watching, you are in your crib again. Thank you, Rodney!

Wagon Train
(1957–65)

A salute to the concept of community, this show reinforces the healing value of close relationships. *Wagon Train* reminds us that only within the circle do we find protection; only together can we make it through the wilderness of human living. And it has even greater relevance to American in the 1990s than it did thirty years ago.

There is much public discourse on the apparent weakening, some would say general collapse, of the American family structure. Many rightly see this as a cause of suffering and pain. Without the nurturing environment of a loving family, people are deprived of a vital element in growth and development. Millions of individuals are indeed so deprived. Self-help and recovery groups have become popular gathering places where individuals find healing and restoration from the deep wounds of a damaged family life. Are we doomed if we have lost this vital experience? No! There is hope for the injured adult, and *Wagon Train* shows us a way.

Throughout the last century, thousands of people set off for the American West to find new opportunities on the golden shores of California. Venturing off into the hostile unknown, families often traveled in groups, forming a "wagon train" that made their journey safer. Under the caring leadership of the good father, wizened wagonmaster Major Seth Adams, families experienced a warm shelter that would have been missing had they made the trek alone. Isn't this life's crucial lesson? The broader the community we join, the stronger our sanctuary as we journey into hostile environments. Solitude is an overrated human need. While our immediate family is important, it is not enough. We must participate in relationships beyond these narrow intimacies. This will deepen our sense of hope that we will reach our destination, reach a land of golden shores, arrive safely and intact as we cross over the mountain.

Wagon Train calls to us: "Come out of yourself. Yes it is difficult to overcome the seduction of aloneness, but that is your depression. Fight the battle. Come out and join the larger family waiting to love and nurture you on your exciting trip across the hostile landscape of human life." *Wagon Train* promises that if you resist the tendency to detach from others and instead join together on the train with other families, in your community, your place of work, your church, you will reap great rewards. Together we can all arrive in a grand and peaceful California!